EASY MAGIC TRICKS

Joseph Leeming

DOVER PUBLICATIONS, INC.
MINEOLA, NEW YORK

Bibliographical Note

Easy Magic Tricks, first published by Dover Publications, Inc., in 2008, is an abridged version of *The Real Book about Magic,* published by Garden City Books, New York, in 1951. Tricks have been omitted from the original text because they are dangerous for children and amateur performers.

Library of Congress Cataloging-in-Publication Data

Leeming, Joseph, 1897–1968.
    [Real Book about Magic]
    Easy magic tricks / Joseph Leeming.
       p. cm.
    Originally published: The Real Book about Magic. Garden City Books : Garden City, New York, 1951.
    ISBN-13: 978-0-486-45555-6
    ISBN-10: 0-486-45555-6
    1. Magic tricks. I. Title.

GV1547.L514 2008
793.8—dc22

2007049444

Manufactured in the United States of America
Dover Publications, Inc., 31 East 2nd Street, Mineola, N.Y. 11501

Contents

1. Magic with Rings

Every person known to be interested in magic is likely to be asked at any time to do some tricks. Or oftentimes a party or group can be entertained with some magic that will baffle the onlookers.

All of the tricks in this book can be done without any expensive or elaborate equipment. However, there are a few simple and proven rules that will add fun to your performance.

Always practice every trick alone or with a trusted friend, until you really know how to do it easily. Then you won't be caught sometime forgetting how a trick is completed.

A part of every magician's equipment is his line of chatter which he keeps up when showing off to the audience. You can't be talking to the audience if you are wondering if your trick will come off, so learn it well before you show it.

When going out on a party, take along a few of the simple things mentioned in this book, so you will have on hand all you need for the tricks you want to do.

The tricks and magic in this book are mostly new and will give everyone a lot of fun.

These tricks are especially good ones to know. You can practically always get hold of one or more rings in any gathering.

Most of the tricks described here are ones that can be done without secret preparation.

1. The Ring Magically Knotted to a String

EFFECT: A spectator is given a piece of string about three feet long and is asked to tie the ends around the magician's wrists. When this has been done, the magician borrows a ring from a member of the audience and turns his back for a moment. When he turns around again, the ring is securely knotted to the middle of the string, which must be cut or untied to remove the ring.

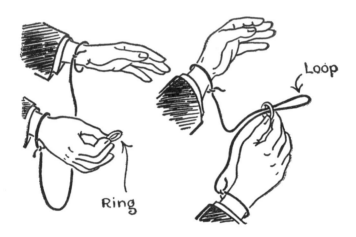

SECRET: The trick is accomplished as follows. Push the center of the length of string hanging between your wrists through the ring, thus forming a loop. Slip this loop over your right hand and wrist, bringing it to a point below the string that already encircles your right wrist. Then pull the loop underneath the string around your wrist and bring it back over your right hand, passing it from the back of the hand to the front. You will find that the ring is firmly knotted then to the middle section of the string between your wrists.

2. The Magically Released Rings

This is one of the most surprising of the impromptu tricks that can be done with rings. It will repay you to master it, as you can do it at any time.

EFFECT: Several rings are borrowed from the audience and the largest is tied to the middle of a piece of string about two feet long. The other rings are then threaded over the two ends of the string by a spectator,

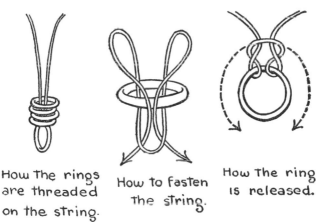

How the rings are threaded on the string.

How to fasten the string.

How the ring is released.

so they rest above the first ring. Two spectators now hold the two ends of the string, and a handkerchief is thrown over the rings. The magician holds his left hand, palm upward, beneath the rings and puts his right hand beneath the handkerchief for a moment. Almost instantly the rings fall down into his left hand, having been magically released from the string.

SECRET: The way in which the first ring is fastened to the center of the string is the secret of the trick. The string is doubled and the looped end is pushed through the ring. The two ends are then passed through the loop

3

and pulled as far as possible, thus securing the ring in a loop. This appears to be a perfectly tight knot, but it can be undone in a moment by simply drawing the loop down over the ring. The string will then pass through the center of the ring, and all the rings will be released and fall into your hand.

3. Instantaneous Ring Release

This is an instantaneous passing of solid through solid, a very surprising effect.

EFFECT: One end of a looped string is passed by the performer through a ring and the other end is then passed

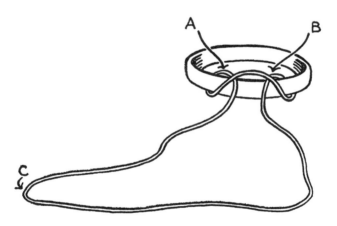

through the first loop. The drawing shows how this is done. Two spectators are then asked to hold the string at the places marked A and B, while the magician grasps the loop at C. The spectators are asked to pull the parts they are holding clear of the ring and to pull on them steadily. The magician, meanwhile, pulls gently but firmly on his part of the string. Now the magician suddenly exclaims, "Pass!" and the ring instantly drops free of the string!

SECRET: You "magically" cause the ring to be released by simply letting go of the part of the string that you are holding. It all happens in a flash and to the audience, it looks as though the string had been drawn right through the solid metal of the ring.

4. The Ring on the String

This is an excellent mystery, for it is worked so quickly that what happens appears to be absolutely impossible.

How did it get
on the string ?

EFFECT: The two ends of a piece of string about eighteen inches long are tied around the performer's wrists. He then takes in one hand a large metal ring or bracelet which the audience has examined to make sure it is solid. The magician turns his back for a moment or steps behind a screen, and reappears immediately with the ring threaded on the string between his wrists.

SECRET: This trick requires a little preparation, for it is done by the use of two identical large metal rings. You can get these at any ten-cent store. Before presenting the trick, slip one of the rings over your right hand and wrist and push it up your arm beneath your coat sleeve so it is well concealed. Now, as soon as you turn your back or step behind a screen, put the other ring in one of your pockets (a vest pocket if you turn your back) and pull the ring on your arm down over your hand and so onto the string.

The beauty of this trick is the speed with which it can be done and a little practice to insure smooth and rapid execution will be well repaid, as the effect is truly startling.

5. The Flying Ring

One of the very best ring tricks, but one that requires thorough practice. Learn it well and you will be able to do it well.

EFFECT: The performer borrows a ring, puts it on his left palm, and closes his hand over it. A handkerchief is then fastened over his closed left hand by a rubber band slipped over hand and wrist. Another handkerchief is then fastened over his right hand in the same way. "Now," says the magician, "I propose to make the ring in my left hand travel up my sleeve, across my chest, and down my right sleeve into my right hand. Which finger of my right hand would you like it to go to?" The audience chooses, say, the first finger. The magician flutters his left fingers, shakes his left arm, moves his shoulders (to help the ring on its way), and then shakes his right arm as the ring travels down it. The rubber band and handkerchief are removed from his left hand, which is found empty. When the handkerchief is removed from his right hand the ring is found on the first finger!

SECRET: As described above, you place the ring on your left palm and close your left hand over it. You must then turn your hand over and raise it chest high, with the

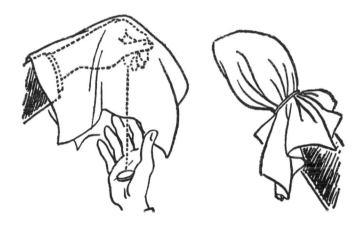

left arm slightly bent. Next ask the audience for a handkerchief and take it in your right hand. Throw it over your closed left hand to completely cover it.

Now take a rubber band placed in readiness on a table or in your right coat pocket and ask a spectator to pass it over the handkerchief down to your wrist. As you make this request, illustrate what you want done with your right hand, passing this hand, with fingers curved inward, underneath the handkerchief toward your left elbow. As the right hand passes beneath the left hand, let the ring drop from the latter into the palm of your right hand. Do not stop the motion of the right hand. Keep it moving slowly and time the drop correctly. This move should be practiced a number of times before a mirror until you can do it smoothly and perfectly, with nothing to indicate what is going on.

Drop your right hand to your side and ask for the loan of a second handkerchief. Meanwhile work the ring into a position at the base of your right second and third fingers. Gripped by the folds of your skin, it can be held tight and will not be visible if you keep your fingers slightly curved inwards. Raise your right hand, palm down, and close your fingers slowly. Have the second handkerchief thrown over your right hand by a spectator and fastened with a rubber band around the wrist. Then proceed to carry the trick out to its conclusion, as outlined above. You will find it easy to work the ring onto the finger chosen by the audience.

6. *The Ring and Pencil Trick*

This trick requires some skill in presentation, but can be mastered with the necessary amount of practice. It is good and has been a favorite with many famous magicians.

EFFECT: The magician borrows a ring and a long pencil or produces a ring and pencil of his own. He wraps the ring in a handkerchief, and then asks a spectator to hold the two ends of the pencil, one in each hand. He asks another spectator to feel the ring inside the handkerchief to be sure it is there, and knocks the ring against the pencil so the other spectators can hear it. Next he puts the handkerchief over and partially around the pencil and pulls it swiftly toward him. As it comes clear of the pencil, the ring is seen to have left the handkerchief and, in some mysterious way, to have gotten onto the pencil.

SECRET: The trick is done with the aid of an extra ring, which you have in a convenient pocket at the beginning. When ready to do the trick, get this ring into your right hand and grip it between the flesh at the roots of the second and third fingers. When your hand is partially closed, it will not be visible to the audience.

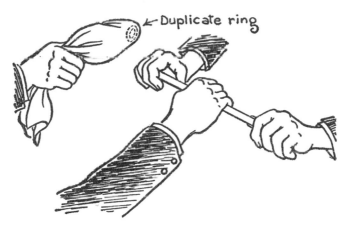

Take the borrowed ring in your right hand, holding it between the tip of the thumb and the tips of the first and second fingers. Spread a handkerchief over your left palm. Then proceed as though to put the borrowed ring in the center of the handkerchief but, instead, drop the concealed ring onto the handkerchief and close your left fingers and thumb around it, concealing the ring inside. At the same time, tuck the borrowed ring into the palm of your right hand.

Take the handkerchief in your right hand and straighten its folds, then put it on the table. Pick up the pencil in your left hand and transfer it to your right hand, sliding it through the center of the ring held in your almost closed right hand. Keep hold of the pencil with your right hand, which is closed around the center portion of the pencil, as in the drawing.

Pick up the handkerchief in your left hand and at the same time ask a spectator to hold the two ends of the pencil. Ask another spectator to feel the ring inside of the handkerchief and then knock it against the pencil.

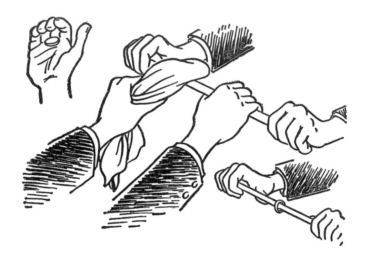

Then let the handkerchief rest on the pencil beside your right hand. Push it over to cover the ring on the pencil, simultaneously taking your right hand from the pencil. Then draw your left hand, still holding the handkerchief, quickly toward you. This will set the borrowed ring spinning around the pencil, and will reveal it to the audience.

While the spectators are still surprised and are removing the borrowed ring from the pencil, quietly remove the extra ring from the handkerchief and drop it in the most convenient pocket. Then pass the handkerchief for examination.

7. The Myslo Ring Flight

EFFECT: The magician slides a ring onto a pencil, covers it with a handkerchief, and asks a spectator to hold the ends of the pencil. He gives an empty, but sealed, envelope to another spectator and asks him to put it in a pocket. He asks the spectator holding the pencil to feel the ring through the handkerchief. It is still there. Presto! The magician draws away the handkerchief and the ring has vanished. He asks the spectator who has the envelope to take it from his pocket and open it. The vanished ring is found inside!

SECRET: For this trick you need three identical rings, which you can get at the ten-cent store. You will also need a secret assistant or confederate in the audience. Cut one of the rings in two and sew one half of it to the center of a handkerchief. Put one of the solid rings in an envelope, which is sealed and given to your confederate, who puts it in his pocket. You are now ready to do the trick.

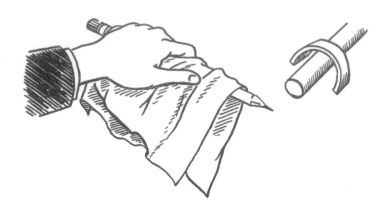

Put the remaining solid ring on a pencil and ask a spectator to hold both ends. Then give an empty sealed envelope to your confederate, who puts it in the pocket already containing the envelope holding the duplicate ring. Throw the handkerchief over the ring, and arrange the half ring sewed to the handkerchief on top of the pencil. Put your right hand under the handkerchief and over the solid ring, and hold the half ring through the handkerchief with your left hand. Ask the spectator holding the pencil to hold the half ring. When he has removed one hand from the pencil to do so, slide your right hand and the solid ring with it to the end he has left free.

Now ask a second spectator to come forward and hold the end of the pencil that is in your right hand. Slip your hand off the pencil and the ring with it. Then remove the handkerchief and reveal that the ring has vanished. The trick ends by the confederate producing the prepared envelope, opening it, and producing the duplicate ring, apparently to his great surprise.

This trick may be done more simply by omitting the confederate and the envelopes. In this case, after you have removed your right hand, and the ring, from the pencil, put your right hand immediately underneath the handkerchief. Tell the audience that you are going to try to make the ring on the pencil "pass!" As you exclaim the word, remove the handkerchief and open your right hand, revealing the ring which in some mysterious way has been freed from the pencil.

8. *Rubbing a Ring onto a Pencil*

This is an excellent trick, but it requires good address and skill in the presentation.

EFFECT: The performer borrows a ring from a spectator and holds it in his left hand. He then asks a spectator to hold both ends of a long pencil. The performer then puts one hand above and one below the pencil and rubs his hands together. The ring is rubbed right onto the center of the pencil.

SECRET: Take the borrowed ring in your right hand. Hold it on your palm and, while showing it to the audience, get it into the position shown in the drawing. A very slight contraction of the hand will then hold it securely. Bring your right hand to the left, turn it over toward your left palm, and pretend to put the ring into your left hand. Close your left fingers at once and keep the hand closed.

Now take a long pencil from your pocket and hold it by the middle with the tips of your right fingers. This will put the lower end of the pencil against the palm, and you will be able without difficulty to slide the ring onto

the pencil. While you do this, tap your left hand with the pencil and talk to the audience, telling them what has happened so far in the trick, etc.

Slide your closed right hand, and the ring with it, to the middle of the pencil and ask a spectator to hold both ends. Put the left hand beneath the pencil, open both hands so the palms come together with the pencil between them, rub the hands together, and then suddenly remove them. The ring will be seen spinning around the pencil, having been magically rubbed through the solid wood.

9. *Instantaneous Flight*

This is an instantaneous and invisible flight of a ring, which has been featured by many famous magicians. Skillfully done, it is a wonderful effect.

14

EFFECT: The magician takes a borrowed ring in his left hand and throws it into the air, where it vanishes, only instantly to reappear on one of the fingers of his right hand.

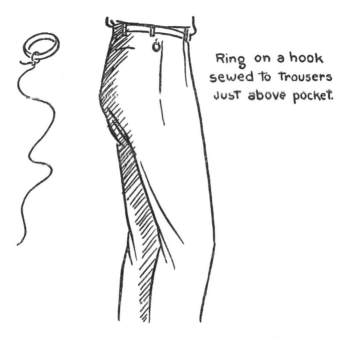

Ring on a hook sewed to Trousers Just above pocket.

SECRET: Two rings are used, which are duplicates. If a ring is borrowed from the audience, which makes the trick more effective, it should be, if possible, a wedding ring, and the performer should provide himself with an imitation wedding ring from the ten-cent store. This ring is tied to one end of a piece of cord, which is led up the left sleeve, across the back, down the right sleeve close to the wrist, where it is tied around the forearm.

The borrowed ring is taken in the right hand and apparently is transferred to the left hand. Actually, however, it is retained in the right hand, tucked away into the

15

space between the thumb and first finger, and the duplicate is shown at the left fingertips. The performer turns his left side toward the audience and hangs the borrowed

How ring is retained
in right hand

ring on a hook of the hook-and-eye variety, which is sewed to the right side of his trousers just above the pocket. The right hand is then shown to be empty.

The last part of the trick is done in a flash. Turn your left side to the audience and get the borrowed ring in your right hand, slipping it over the tip of the second finger. Face the audience and point to the ring in your left hand with your right forefinger, keeping the other fingers closed. Throw both hands upward, and let go of the ring in your left hand. It will fly up your left sleeve. At the same instant open the fingers of your right hand and look upward at it. The ring will be seen to have flown to your right second finger.

2. Impromptu Coin Tricks

1. *The Multiplying Penny*

EFFECT: This is a new method of doubling your money, which takes only an instant to carry out. The magician holds a penny between his right thumb and forefinger and shows it to the audience. He takes it in his left hand, exhibits it, and returns it to his right hand. He then places it on the palm of his left hand and rubs it with his right fingertips. It is suddenly seen to double itself, there being two pennies in the left hand.

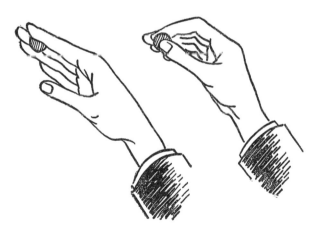

SECRET: The moves in the trick are described above. Have two pennies in your right trouser pocket before commencing. Remove them both with your right hand, clipping one of them between the tips of your first and second fingers while your hand is still in the pocket. Practice this a few times and it will be easy to do smoothly. Bring the other penny out, held between the tip of your thumb and first finger. Take it in your left hand immediately, and pass it back and forth between your hands a few times, showing it to the audience, while you tell them it is a magic penny.

Put the visible penny squarely on the center of your left palm. Then rub it with your right fingertips and as you do so let the hidden penny drop into your left palm. Make a few more rubs, remove the right hand, and close the left. Then open the left hand to show the two pennies.

2. *The Flying Coins*

This is an easily executed coin flight, but it is as impressive in effect as many other more elaborate tricks of the same nature.

EFFECT: The magician wraps a penny in a handkerchief and gives it to a spectator to hold. He then wraps up a nickel in a second handkerchief, which he hands to a second spectator. "Watch closely, now," he says. "Perhaps you can see the coins flying through the air. Pass!" The spectators unfold the handkerchiefs and the coins are found to have changed places.

SECRET: The secret lies in the use of two nickels. You conceal one of these in your right hand, gripping it at the base of your thumb, before commencing the trick. The other nickel and the penny are placed on a table in full view.

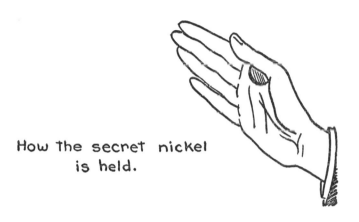

How the secret nickel is held.

Pick up the penny in your right hand, place it in the center of a handkerchief, and pretend to wrap it up. Before folding over part of the handkerchief, however, drop the concealed nickel into it and remove the penny, tucking it into the place previously occupied by the nickel. Give the handkerchief to a spectator, and say, "Will you please hold this handkerchief, which contains the penny?"

Now pick up the nickel from the table and pretend to wrap it up in a second handkerchief, but substitute the concealed penny for it in the same way that the previous change was effected. When the handkerchiefs are unfolded, the coins will have mysteriously changed places.

3. Rubbing a Coin into Invisibility

This trick will be found useful when you are unexpectedly called on to "do some magic" and are unprepared for anything elaborate. The effect is good, and it is well worth learning.

EFFECT: A coin is borrowed and the performer, holding it in his left fingertips, rubs it against his right coat sleeve just above the elbow, the elbow being rested on a table, with the performer seated. If no table is handy, you can stand and hold the right forearm vertical. Soon the heat induced by the rubbing, or so the performer says, gradually melts the metal and the coin vanishes into thin air.

SECRET: After rubbing the coin back and forth

against your coat sleeve several times, it is dropped, as if by accident, on the table or floor. The right hand picks it up and apparently places it in the left, but it is really retained in the right hand, gripped at the base of the thumb. The left fingers are immediately placed against the coat sleeve and moved briskly up and down until you are ready to reveal the coin's disappearance.

A good way to end this trick is to immediately show your right, as well as your left hand, empty. To do this, tuck the coin inside your shirt collar while the final rubbing procedure is going on.

4. The Traveling Coins

This is a very deceptive trick, which is apparently done by means of a clever substitution, or so the audience is led to believe, but which really requires no sleight of hand at all. It requires two or three seconds of secret preparation, but this is so slight that it is classed here as an impromptu trick.

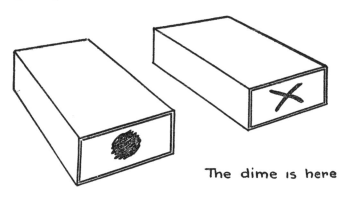

The dime is here

The quarter is here.

EFFECT: A quarter and a dime are borrowed from the audience. The quarter is put in a small wooden match box or other small box and a circle is marked with pencil, ink, or crayon on one end of the box. The dime is then put in another match box, on one end of which is marked an X. The two boxes are placed on the table, the magician then pronounces the magic word of power, "Pass!" and upon opening the boxes, the coins are found to have

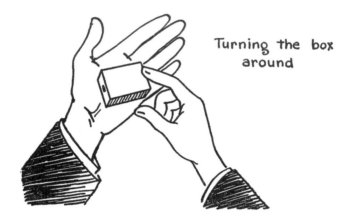

Turning the box around

changed places. The quarter is in the box marked with an X and the dime in the box marked with a circle.

SECRET: Before doing the trick, mark two match boxes, one with an X and one with a circle. The marks are put on one end of each box and the marked ends are, of course, not shown to the audience. In doing the trick, put the quarter in the box marked with an X and then draw a circle on the opposite end in full view of the audience. Put the dime in the other box and draw an X on the end toward the audience.

Before you put each box on the table, you must turn it around to show the secretly made marks. With a small match box this is easy. Simply hold it in your left hand while talking to the audience, curling the fingers in to partially conceal the box from the audience. With your right hand you can turn the box around without fear of detection.

5. *The Coin in the Glass*

EFFECT: The magician puts a coin in the center of a handkerchief that is spread out flat on the table. He

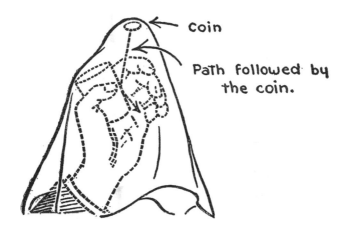

then takes a small glass in his left hand and, picking up the coin and the handkerchief, places the coin over the glass, with the folds of the handkerchief hanging down and concealing it from the view of the audience. He drops the coin into the glass and everybody hears it tinkle as he does so. When the handkerchief is removed from the glass, however, the coin has disappeared.

SECRET: Actually, the coin is never dropped into the

glass at all. It is dropped against the side of the glass and this contact makes exactly the same sound as if it had dropped right into the glass. After striking the side of the glass, the coin drops down into the left hand, and is kept concealed in this hand as long as required. The attention of the audience is diverted from the left hand by lifting the covered glass with your right hand and putting it on a table, to rest there until you are ready to remove the handkerchief and disclose the coin's disappearance. Meanwhile you can turn your right side to the audience and slip the coin into a left-hand pocket.

6. The "Tapping Pencil" Coin Trick

This is a professional effect, which will require careful practice. It is not hard to do, but is so good that it should be well rehearsed in order to get the full effect.

EFFECT: The magician places a half dollar in his right hand, which he closes. He takes a pencil from his pocket and taps his right hand, then opens his hand, and the coin has vanished. He closes his hand again and once more taps it with the pencil. When he opens his hand, the coin has reappeared. Well done, this trick will make your reputation.

SECRET: The only preparation needed is to put a pencil in your right-hand upper vest pocket or your inside coat pocket.

Borrow a half dollar or produce one of your own and, if you wish, have it marked with a pencil to identify it. Put it in your left hand at the base of your first finger (see drawing). Then put it in your right palm by turning your left hand over and letting the coin drop out of it. Hold your hands close together.

Take the pencil from your pocket and tap your closed right hand. Open your hand. The coin is still there. "Well, that's funny," you say. "We'd better try it again." Put the pencil back in your pocket. Then put the coin in your left hand, in the same position as before.

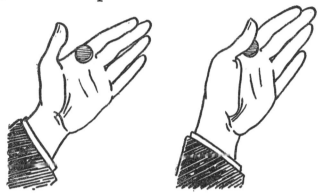

Now, you apparently put the coin back into your right hand. Actually, however, you put your left thumb against it, just as you start to turn your left hand over (see drawing). This holds the coin firmly and easily in the left hand. Close your right fingers, as though the hand were holding the coin.

Take out the pencil again with your left hand and, as you do so, drop the coin into the top of your right coat sleeve. Your right arm is bent, so the coin will drop down only as far as your elbow. Now tap your closed right hand with the pencil, open it up, and show that the coin has vanished.

Hold the pencil up in your left hand and say, "The magic is all in the pencil. It's better than any magic word!" At the same time, drop your right hand down to your side and catch in it the coin, which will fall down your sleeve. Close your hand and bring it up in front of

you again. Tap your right hand again, open it up, and show that the coin has reappeared.

7. *Multiplying Pennies*

This is an excellent impromptu trick, if you have *practiced it well*. It requires a little skill and a little deftness in execution.

EFFECT: Three pennies are borrowed from the audience and placed in the performer's right hand. Tossing them into his left hand, he shows that there are still three pennies only. After tossing them back and forth several times, the magician keeps them in his left hand, which he closes and asks the audience how many pennies he has. The answer is bound to be "Three," but when the hand is opened, it is seen to contain four pennies.

SECRET: Four pennies are used for the trick. One of them is placed in the left hand before the commencement of the trick, being nipped between the first and sec-

ond fingers. The fingers are curled slightly inward. When the three pennies borrowed from the audience are placed in the right hand, one of them is also nipped between the fingers in the same way, so that it can be held onto or released, just as you wish. The other two pennies are held loose in the right palm.

In tossing the (presumably) three pennies from hand to hand, only two are actually tossed each time. Thus there are always three pennies to be shown in either hand. Show the three pennies two or three times, toss the pennies back and forth a few more times, and then bring the trick to its conclusion.

8. The Coins in the Hat

EFFECT: A coin is borrowed from the audience and marked with a pencil so that it can be identified. It is then dropped into a hat in which a number of other coins of the same value (all pennies, for example) have previously been placed. The magician reaches into the hat and picks out the marked coin.

SECRET: The trick requires a somewhat delicate sense of touch, but can be done easily after a little practice. The extra coins, four or five in number, are first placed in the hat. The other coin is then marked and passed around the audience so that everyone can see the mark. If there are only one or two spectators you can ask one of them to hold the marked coin in his closed hand for a few minutes to magnetize it. During the procedure the spectator's hand warms the coin and it can be detected at once by the sense of touch. Reach into the hat and remove the coins one at a time. When you pick up the marked one, you will be able to tell the difference at once.

9. The Coin in the Sleeve

EFFECT: In this trick the performer tells the audience that he is going to do, openly and without deception, what magicians are so often accused of doing in secret, namely, put something up his sleeve. Suiting his actions to his words, he drops a quarter into his left sleeve. Bringing his left hand down, he shakes his arm as though to shake out the coin, but no coin appears. It has disappeared completely.

SECRET: The quarter is held in the right hand and is not dropped into the left sleeve at all, but into the left breast or handkerchief pocket of your coat. The left fore-

arm is held upright so the hand is almost level with the face. In this position it conceals the pocket. The quarter is held between the right thumb and forefinger. Just before it is dropped into the pocket, the other fingers of the right hand are inserted into the sleeve, ostensibly to open it up. Actually this movement covers the dropping of the coin into your pocket. You then immediately put your right thumb and forefinger into your sleeve and announce, "There you see, I have dropped the coin down my sleeve." Then continue to the end of the trick.

3. Coin Tricks Requiring Simple Apparatus

The tricks in this lesson are of various kinds—some for informal parlor entertainment, others that can well be included in a prepared magic show. None of them are really difficult.

1. The Handkerchief Coin Vanish

EFFECT: A coin is wrapped in a handkerchief and, at the magician's command, disappears.

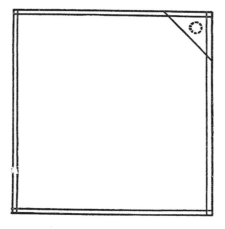

SECRET: This is one of the best and simplest means by which a coin can be vanished without the use of sleight of hand. A handkerchief is prepared by concealing a penny in one corner, sewing over it a piece of material similar to that of which the handkerchief is made. The coin to be vanished—a penny, nickel, or dime, usually—is apparently placed in the center of the handkerchief, which is spread over your left palm, and wrapped up. Actually, you retain the coin in your right hand and wrap up the concealed coin. The spectators can now feel the coin in the handkerchief, or a spectator may even hold the handkerchief, for "safe keeping." If the latter is done, the magician takes one corner of the handkerchief, when the time arrives to show that the coin has vanished, and shakes the handkerchief out, the spectator releasing his hold.

2. The Paper Cone and Coin

EFFECT: The magician rolls a piece of newspaper into a cone, which he places point downward in a drinking glass. Picking up a coin, he causes it to vanish. He then lifts up the paper cone and inverts it, and the coin falls out of it, into the glass.

SECRET: The newspaper is prepared by pasting to it, near its center, a small piece cut from another newspaper. This piece should be just large enough to form a pocket in which the coin to be used will fit comfortably. It is

Secret
Pocket in
newspaper

pasted around three sides only, the top being left open, and a duplicate coin is tucked into the pocket before the performance. The other coin is vanished by the "Handkerchief Coin Vanish." Keep it in your hand until there is a convenient opportunity to put it in one of your pockets.

3. Fingertip Coin Magic

EFFECT: The performer borrows half a dozen pennies from spectators and drops them one at a time into a hat. He reads aloud the date on each penny before dropping it and a spectator writes down the dates. The performer shakes the coins in the hat to mix them up and then takes them out and drops them into the inside breast pocket of his coat. People in the audience are then asked to name one of the dates and the magician at once produces the penny bearing that date from his pocket. The trick can be continued by producing one or two more pennies or all of them as the dates are given by the audience from among those written down.

SECRET: Before doing the trick put six pennies of your own in your upper right-hand vest pocket. Memorize the dates on these pennies and arrange them in order so you can instantly pick out any one of them. When you pretend to read the dates on the borrowed pennies, you really call out the dates on the pennies in your vest

pocket. When the spectators call the dates, stand with your right side to the audience and hold your right coat lapel with your right hand, holding the coat slightly open. When a date is called, put your left hand into your vest pocket and bring out the right coin.

4. *The Mysto Coin Vanish*

EFFECT: A coin is shown to the audience and the performer, holding it in his left hand, throws a handker-

Yes it's there

chief over it. Spectators are asked to put their hands beneath the handkerchief and feel the coin, which they do. All agree that it is there, but when the performer removes the handkerchief, the coin has vanished in the twinkling of an eye.

Where did it go?

SECRET: This is a splendid trick, and one that is practically 100 per cent undetectable. A friend is needed to act as a secret confederate. He is the last spectator to put his hand beneath the handkerchief, and as he does so, he picks up the coin and removes it, hidden between his thumb and fingers.

4. Mathematical Magic

"Mathematical Magic" is one of the most useful and entertaining branches of the magician's repertoire. These tricks can, for the most part, be done on the spur of the moment and are always valuable to use to provide variety between other effects such as card, coin, or handkerchief tricks. Some of the most baffling mathematical or number tricks are described in this lesson.

1. Lightning Addition

EFFECT: The performer asks the audience to write down two rows of figures, each row containing five figures, as:

2, 3, 6, 9, 7
4, 1, 6, 5, 2

The performer then puts down a third row of figures, the audience a fourth, and the performer a fifth. Glancing at the figures for a brief moment, the performer writes something on a piece of paper which he folds and gives to a spectator to hold. "This is an example of instant calculation," he says. "Will you now add up the five figures we have written down and call out the total?" This is done and after the total has been announced, the performer's piece of paper is unfolded. On it is written the correct total, which has just been added up and called out by the spectator.

SECRET: When you write down the third and fifth rows of figures, you put down numbers that will total 9 when added to the number just above. Thus, if the second row were 4, 1, 6, 5, 2, as above, you would write 5, 8, 3, 4, 7 for the third line. The 4 and 5, 1 and 8, 6 and 3, 5 and 4, and 2 and 7 all total 9.

If this is done, the grand total can always be discerned in a flash by subtracting 2 from the right-hand number of the first line and placing 2 in front of the first number of the first line.

Here is an example:

$$
\begin{array}{l}
\text{Audience writes} - 2, 3, 6, 9, 7 \\
\text{Audience writes} - 4, 1, 6, 5, 2 \\
\text{Performer writes} - 5, 8, 3, 4, 7 \\
\text{Audience writes} - 8, 4, 3, 2, 1 \\
\text{Performer writes} - 1, 5, 6, 7, 8 \\
\hline
\text{Total} \qquad 2\ 2\ 3,\ 6\ 9\ 5
\end{array}
$$

2. The Canceled Number

EFFECT: A spectator is asked to write down a figure containing as many numbers as he wishes, such as, say, 3 2 6 4 5. He is then to add the numbers together. This done, the performer asks him to subtract the sum of the numbers from the original figure and then to cancel out any number he wishes from the remainder. The figures left are then added together, and their sum is told to the performer, who at once tells what number was canceled out.

SECRET: To determine the canceled number, all you have to do is subtract the final sum told you by the spectator from the next higher multiple of 9. If the sum itself is a multiple of 9, no subtraction is necessary, for 9 was the figure canceled.

Suppose the original number to be 3 2 6 4 5. The individual numbers added together make 20, which is subtracted from the original number, leaving 3 2 6 2 5. The spectator cancels 6, let us say, and adds the remaining numbers 3, 2, 2, 5, which total 12. He tells you this figure. The multiple of 9 next higher than 12 is 18, so you subtract 12 from 18. This gives you 6, which is the canceled number.

3. The Telepathic Total

EFFECT: The magician asks a spectator to write a five-number figure on a piece of paper. He then asks the spectator to write this number in reverse order underneath the first figure and to subtract the smaller of the two numbers from the larger. The number thus obtained is reversed and added to the remainder obtained by the subtraction. The performer asks the spectator to concentrate on the last figure obtained. After a moment or two he gets it by means of telepathy, or so he says, and announces what it is.

SECRET: This trick sounds a little complicated, but an example will show that it is easy to do and to remember how to do. Assume that the spectator wrote the number 2 3 6 7 8. He reverses this, making 8 7 6 3 2, and subtracts the smaller from the larger figure thus:

$$
\begin{array}{r}
8\ 7\ 6\ 3\ 2 \\
-2\ 3\ 6\ 7\ 8 \\
\hline
6\ 3\ 9\ 5\ 4
\end{array}
$$

He then reverses the remainder, 6 3 9 5 4, making
4 5 9 3 6, and adds it thus:

$$
\begin{array}{r}
6\ 3\ 9\ 5\ 4 \\
4\ 5\ 9\ 3\ 6 \\
\hline
1\ 0\ 9,8\ 9\ 0
\end{array}
$$

In practically every instance the total will be 1 0 9, 8 9 0,
no matter what original number is used. All you have to
do to divine the number "by telepathy" is to assume the
number 109,890. Once in a great while the total will come
out 99,099 and, if your first total (109,890) proves to be
wrong, all you have to do is pretend to think for a moment
and then announce the total to be 99,099.

4. Birthday Magic

EFFECT: This is a mathematical method of deter-
mining the month and year of anyone's birthday. It is
sometimes next to impossible to get people to tell their
age, but by using this method you can find it out without
their even knowing it.

SECRET: Ask the person to think of the number of
the month in which his birthday occurs, counting January
as 1, February as 2, and so on. Then tell him to multiply
this number by 2, add 5, multiply the product by 50, and
then add his age. From the total he is to subtract 365 and
add 115. The last two numbers of this final number will

be the person's age, and the first number or numbers will denote the month in which he was born.

Assume a 20-year-old person born in January, and the figuring is as follows:

Multiply 1 (for January) by 2=	2
Add 5	5
	7
Multiply by 50	350
Add age	20
	370
Subtract 365	5
Add 115	120

The first number, 1, shows that his birthday falls in January. The remaining numbers, 20, reveal his age.

5. Important Dates

EFFECT: The magician asks a spectator to write down the year of his birth and then the year in which some other important event happened, such as his marriage or his graduation from school or college. Under these two dates he is asked to write his age at the end of the current year. This is not necessarily his age at the time the trick is being done, but it is his age as of the following December 31. One more figure is added and it is the number of years that have elapsed since the year in which the important event happened.

While the spectator is adding these figures, the magician scribbles a number on a piece of paper, which he gives to another spectator to hold. When the total of the spectator's figures is added up, the magician's paper is unfolded and is found to have the correct total written on it.

SECRET: This requires no difficult figuring at all, since the answer will always be double the number of the year in which the trick is done.

Here is an example for the year 1945:

Birth year	1925
Important event in	1940
Age	20
Years since important event	5
Total	3890=2 x 1945

6. Counting to One Hundred

This is one of the most perplexing of all tricks having to do with numbers. Once you have mastered the simple technique, it will always puzzle your friends.

EFFECT: Two people, one of whom is the magician, count to 100, observing certain rules. The first person is to call out a number between 1 and 10, inclusive. The second person is also to call out a number between 1 and 10. This is continued until one person or the other is able to add a number that brings the total up to exactly 100. The magician always wins.

SECRET: To be sure to win, you must always be the one to call out 89. Then, no matter what number between 1 and 10 is added by your opponent, it will not bring the total up to 100. If, for example, he added the highest number allowed, namely 10, it would make the total 99, and by adding 1, you would make it 100 and win.

You should bear in mind the figure 78, for by naming this figure you can always make 89 your own as well. If the precaution regarding calling out 78 is not taken, it is sometimes possible for the other person to hit on 89.

7. Telling a Number Thought of

This is one of the simplest methods of discovering a number thought of by a spectator. A feat of this kind is not important as a single trick, but it is very useful as one of the many unexpected and surprising bits of magic with which you can amuse your friends and show them varying facts of your knowledge of magic.

EFFECT: Ask a spectator to think of a number. Then tell him to double it, multiply the sum by 5, and tell you the product. You then tell him at once what number he thought of.

SECRET: The number thought of will be the last number arrived at, with its right-hand figure, which will always be a 5 or a 0, removed.

Thus, if the person thought of the number 10, doubling it would make 20, and multiplying it by 5 would make 100. Cut off the right-hand figure, which in this case is a 0, and the original number, 10, is left.

8. All Alike

EFFECT: The magician gives a pad and pencil to one of the spectators and asks him to write down the digits starting with the figure 1 and continuing up to 9, but leaving out 8. He is to write, that is: 1, 2, 3, 4, 5, 6, 7, 9. The magician then asks some other member of the audience to choose one of the numbers that has been written down. Suppose it is 2. The magician names another number and asks the first spectator to write it down on the pad and multiply his first number—1, 2, 3, 4, 5, 6, 7, 9— by it. He tells the spectator the answer will be a very surprising one, and so it is, for it consists entirely of 2's, one after the other.

SECRET: When the second spectator chooses his number you multiply it by 9 and give the resulting number to the spectator to use as his multiplier. In the case cited, multiply 2 by 9 to get 18, and the multiplication is as follows:

$$
\begin{array}{r}
12345679 \\
18 \\
\hline
98765432 \\
12345679 \\
\hline
222,222,222
\end{array}
$$

The trick works the same way whatever number is chosen. The answer, that is, will always consist of the chosen number only.

9. The Number in the Envelope

EFFECT: The magician takes a piece of paper and, with an air of deep concentration, writes something on it. He then puts the paper in an envelope, which he seals. Members of the audience are asked to call out numbers between 1 and 10 and as each number is called the magician writes it down on the envelope. After half a dozen or so numbers have been written down, the magician draws a line beneath the column, and hands the envelope to a spectator with the request that he add the numbers. This done, the spectator is asked to open the envelope and read what is written on the paper. There is a number on the paper, and it is the total of the column of figures. The magician, by his mysterious control over other people's minds, has forced the spectators to call out the numbers that would add up to the sum he wrote on the paper at the beginning of the trick.

SECRET: For a simply executed trick this is one that is really baffling. First, you must decide on a number between 35 and 45, say 42, and write it in front of the audience on the paper that is to be put in the envelope. A number of this size is chosen because if seven or eight numbers between 1 and 10 are called out at random, they will usually add up to a total somewhere between 35 and 45.

Having sealed the paper bearing the number 42 in the envelope, proceed to write down the audience's numbers as they are called out, adding them up mentally as you write them down. Leave a space after the second figure. You will put a number of your own in it in a moment. When your mental total approaches 42, tell the audience that you have enough numbers and, after you write the last number, add another that will bring the total up to 42, putting it in the space left below the second number. Then hand the envelope to a spectator and let the trick come to its conclusion.

An example of how the trick works is given:

Audience's Number	You Add Mentally	At the End Add
3		
8	11	
		5
7	18	
4	22	
9	31	
6	37—Then add 5, putting it in	

the space left open for it.

10. *The Telephone Book Test*

This is an outstanding number mystery that is a favorite with many professional magicians.

EFFECT: The performer gives one of the spectators a telephone book and then takes from his table a pad and pencil. He asks the spectator to call out any three single numbers, such as 4, 7, and 2, and writes these down, one after the other in a horizontal line. The pad is then given to a spectator, who is asked to reverse the numbers, to obtain in this case 274, and to subtract the smaller number from the larger. When this has been done, he is asked to reverse the answer and to add the number thus obtained to the answer. The process is as follows:

The first number is	472
Reversed, it is	274
Smaller subtracted from larger	198
Answer reversed and added	891
Total	1089

The total is 1089. The magician asks the person who has the telephone book to turn to page 10 and count to the 89th name. When he has done so, he is asked to concentrate on it very deeply. The magician also concentrates, to exercise his telepathic powers, and after a few moments writes something on a piece of paper, which he folds and hands to a spectator.

"Will you please read out the 89th name," he asks the man with the book. This is done and the name is, say, Bannerman.

"Now will you please unfold the paper and read the message I received from this gentleman." The person holding the paper unfolds it and reads the word "Bannerman," and also the initials, street address and telephone number.

SECRET: The trick is done by forcing the 89th name on the tenth page of the phone book. If you have a large book you can force the ninth name on page 108, or, by using a novel you can force the ninth line on page 108. This is so, because the answer obtained will always be 1089.

There is only one thing to watch out for. If the answer to the subtraction (198 in the example above) consists of only two figures, add a zero at the left. Should this number be, for example, 98, tell the spectator to put a zero in front of it and then reverse this number to form 890.

5. Magic with Handkerchiefs

Two kinds of handkerchiefs are used by magicians—the ordinary kind that we all carry around, and the smaller white or brightly colored "silks" which we have all seen magicians employ. Silks can be purchased at all magic-supply houses and it is recommended that you get several of them. They are needed for the tricks described in this lesson. The following lesson is devoted to tricks done with ordinary handkerchiefs.

1. Handkerchief from Nowhere

This is a good trick with which to introduce a series of three or four handkerchief effects. It takes only a moment

or two of preparation and is as effective an "appearance" as any in the book.

EFFECT: The magician shows that both of his hands are empty and pulls up his sleeves to demonstrate that there is nothing concealed in them. He then puts his two hands together and shakes them gently up and down. A brightly colored handkerchief emerges slowly from between his hands.

SECRET: The trick is done by rolling up a "silk" or small ordinary handkerchief into as small a compass as possible and secretly tucking it into the crook of the right elbow, hiding it from sight by a fold of the coat sleeve.

By holding your arm slightly bent, the handkerchief can easily be kept in place and out of sight.

After showing both hands empty, pull up your coat sleeves, first the left and then the right. As you pull up the right sleeve, grasping it at the elbow, remove the handkerchief from its hiding place and hold it concealed in the left hand. Then bring your two hands together and move them up and down, allowing the handkerchief to appear little by little from between them.

2. Vanishing a Handkerchief

EFFECT: The performer takes a handkerchief, holds it between both hands, and moves his hands slowly up and down, drawing the handkerchief into the space between his hands as he does so. Gradually the handker-

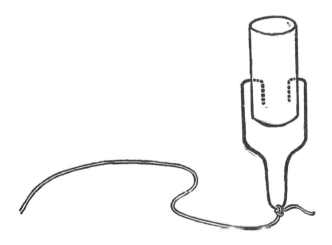

chief is seen to get smaller and smaller until finally the magician spreads his hands apart and they are seen to be empty.

SECRET: The most usual way of vanishing a handkerchief is by means of a gimmick known as a handkerchief "pull." These can be purchased at magic-supply stores or can be made at home. A pull is simply a small receptacle attached to a length of elastic cord, so arranged that when a handkerchief is pushed into the receptacle and the latter is released, the elastic will draw the pull under your coat. A good homemade pull can be made with a piece of cardboard mailing tube about ¾ inch in diameter and 1 inch long. Into this little tube fit a hairpin or a piece of wire, as shown in the drawing, and tie the elastic cord to this wire.

How elastic cord pull is carried.

One end of the elastic cord is tied around a suspender button or belt loop on the left side of the body, first passing it through a right-hand belt loop or a loop of cloth sewed to the trousers at the point indicated in the drawing. This loop will keep the pull from dropping down into sight beneath your coat, and will also keep it where you can easily get hold of it. When you are ready to get hold of it, you must turn your left side to the audience while you are secretly getting possession of the pull with your right hand.

Arrange the length of the elastic cord so that the pull can be drawn outwards from the body about fifteen inches, with sufficient tension to make it fly back instantly under your coat when it is released.

A piece of stout string can be used instead of elastic cord, if the latter is not available. Tie the free end of the string around your left wrist and carry the string from there up your left arm, across your back beneath your vest, and out through the right armhole of the vest. The pull will then hang down from the armhole and will be hidden by your coat.

When vanishing a handkerchief, turn your left side to the audience and get the pull in your right hand. Hold the handkerchief in your left hand. Turn your right side to the audience, put your hands together, and push the handkerchief slowly into the pull. When it is well inside, spread your arms quickly apart and upward. This will draw the pull instantly out of sight beneath your coat.

3. *The Color-Changing Handkerchief*

EFFECT: This is one of the most beautiful of all handkerchief sleights and is an effect that is used by all professional magicians. In performing it, the magician pushes a red silk handkerchief into his closed right hand. As it passes through his hand it changes color and emerges at the bottom a green.

SECRET: The trick is done with the aid of a handkerchief pull made of a cardboard mailing tube. It is prepared by putting a green silk handkerchief inside it, and is arranged as above so the right hand can get hold of it easily.

When doing the trick, get the pull into your right hand. Then take the red silk in your left hand and push it slowly

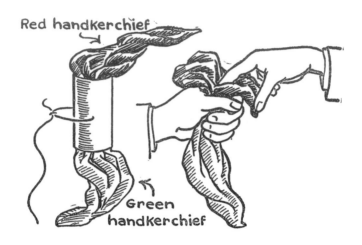

Red handkerchief

Green handkerchief

down into your right hand. As it goes into your hand, it enters the top of the pull and pushes out the green handkerchief. When the red silk is all inside the pull, remove the green silk with your left hand and hold it up, displaying it to the audience. While they are gazing at it, release the pull, and then show the right hand empty.

4. The Handkerchief Dye Tube

EFFECT: This is a more elaborate version of the colorchanging handkerchief trick. In the present trick, three white silks are pushed through a tube made in front of the audience from a piece of stiff paper. When the silks emerge, they are dyed three different colors, as red, yellow, and blue.

SECRET: The trick is done with the aid of a gimmick which is shown in the drawing. This is a piece of 1½-inch-diameter mailing tube about 3 inches long. Inside it is glued a piece of tape as shown. Before doing the trick,

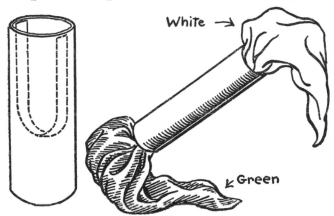

the three colored silks are pushed into the tube. The tape keeps them from going all the way through.

Put the tube on your table and put the three white silks on top of it. Near by put a piece of stiff paper measuring about 12 inches square.

When doing the trick, first pick up the piece of paper and show it, front and back, to the audience. Then hold the paper in your right hand and lower it to the table to a point right beside the white silks. With your left hand pick up the white silks and simultaneously move the paper over to cover the tube containing the colored silks.

After showing the white silks, put them down on the table. Pick up the square of paper and with it pick up the tube, keeping it back of the paper. Then roll up the paper to form a tube around the small secret tube.

Hold the paper tube in your left hand and put the white silks into it one by one. Push these silks down into the tube with a wand or with a pencil. As they enter the hidden tube they force out the colored handkerchiefs, which emerge slowly from the bottom of the tube. Pull these out with your right hand and, as soon as you remove the last one, loosen the grasp of your left-hand fingers on the tube and allow the small tube to fall into your right hand. Put the last handkerchief and the small tube on your table and, with both hands free, unroll the paper tube and show it front and back.

5. *Flying Handkerchiefs*

EFFECT: With the aid of the simple piece of equipment described here, you can do a number of very surprising vanishing and reappearing handkerchief tricks. A piece of paper is rolled into a cone or cornucopia shape and a handkerchief is placed inside it. Presto! When the cone is opened up, the handkerchief has disappeared. A handkerchief placed in one cone can be made to vanish and reappear in another cone. A handkerchief placed in a cone can be made to change colors. Other effects will doubtless occur to you as you experiment with the paper cones used for this trick.

SECRET: Ordinary newspaper is the best material to use for the cones. A double sheet of two pages is folded over on the creased center line and the edges are pasted together with the exception of a little space along the top near one corner, where the paper is left unpasted so as to form a little pocket just large enough to contain a lady's handkerchief or a magician's silk. To the audience the paper looks like a single sheet torn from a newspaper.

To vanish a silk, it is simply put into the little pocket after the paper is rolled up. To transfer a silk from one cone to another, a second piece of paper is prepared as

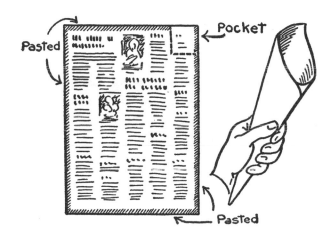

described and a duplicate handkerchief is hidden in the pocket before showing the trick. To make a handkerchief change color, a piece of paper is prepared with two hidden pockets, and the second handkerchief is concealed in one of them before the performance.

6. Twentieth-Century Silks

EFFECT: The performer ties together a red and a green silk handkerchief and drops them into a hat that is on his table. He then takes a white silk and causes it to vanish. Reaching into the hat, he withdraws from it the red and green silks with the white one tied in between them.

SECRET: You will need for this trick six silks—two red, two green, and two white—a hat, and a handkerchief pull.

To prepare for the trick, tie one of the white silks between a red and green one. Roll these up into a small bundle and put them under the sweatband of the hat. Put the hat on your table, crown downwards. Put the three duplicate silks on your table close to the hat.

Pick up the hat and show it to be empty, grasping it with your fingers inside and covering the band where the silks are hidden. Put the hat back on the table, mouth upwards, and as you do so, lift the sweatband with your fingers so the silks will fall inside the hat.

Now pick up the red and green silks that are on the table, tie them together, and drop them into the hat. Take the white silk from the table and vanish it by means of the handkerchief pull, which you have in readiness beneath your coat. Then put your hand into the hat, grasp

one corner of the knotted silks, and bring them out, revealing the white silk tied between the red and green ones.

56

There is a possibility that the audience will wish to examine the hat at the end of the trick. If they do so, the red and green silks inside it must be removed and the removal must be carried out in a manner that will not incite suspicion. The best way is probably as follows: when you put the knotted red and green silks into the hat, roll them up into a fairly compact bundle. Then, after removing the three knotted silks and holding them aloft in your left hand, bring them over to the hat and

drop them in front of it. Under this cover, put your right hand in the hat and tuck the other two silks underneath the sweatband. Casually show your right hand empty and say, "The hat, of course, is empty. I had better show you so you can see for yourselves." Pick up the hat as before and show it to be empty.

7. *The Penetrating Silk*

This is a handkerchief trick that is outstanding in effect. It requires very little skill and careful practice will make it a real illusion.

EFFECT: The performer rolls a green silk into a ball and drops it into a drinking glass. He then puts a red bandana handkerchief over the glass and twists its ends around the bottom of the glass, where he holds them, at the same time securing the bandana in place with a rubber band. In a moment a miracle happens. The green silk emerges through the center of the bandana where it is stretched over the top of the glass. When the green silk has passed completely through, the bandana is removed from the glass. The glass is empty and the bandana and the green silk are passed for examination.

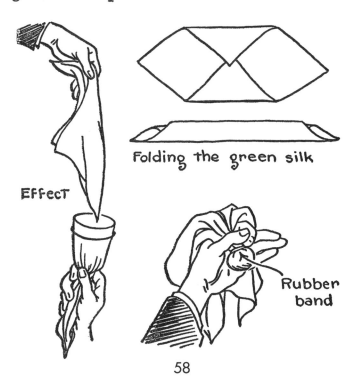

Folding the green silk

Effect

Rubber band

58

SECRET: For this trick you will need two green silks, a red bandana handkerchief, two rubber bands, and a bottomless drinking glass. It is best to buy the bottomless glass from a magic-supply dealer (usually about 75 cents), but it is possible to have a hardware-store glazier make one for you.

Put one of the green silks on the table and fold two corners into the center, fold each side in half again to the center, until the silk is in the form of a strip about 1½ inches wide. Put the bandana over your left fist and push down the center to make a little well. Put one end of the folded silk into this well, and then push the rest of it in, so the opposite end will be at the top. Press the silk down tightly and then put a small rubber band around the bandana to hold the silk in place, as shown in the drawings.

Put the bottomless glass on your table beside the second green silk. Put the second rubber band, which should be large enough to go around the glass, in your left trouser pocket.

Now to do the trick. Show the green silk to the audience and then roll it into a ball, tucking one end into the folds to keep it from unrolling. Pick up the glass with your left hand and drop the silk into it. The glass is put on the palm of your hand so the silk will not drop right through it. Take the bandana in your right hand, with the hidden silk to the rear, and throw it over the glass so that the bundle containing the silk is within the glass.

Arrange the bandana around the glass and take both in your right hand, leaving the rolled-up green silk in your left palm. Put your left hand into your left trouser pocket. Leave the silk in it and immediately bring out the rubber band. Put it around the glass to hold the bandana in place. Twist the ends of the bandana at the bottom of the glass and hold them in your right hand, steadying the glass with your left hand.

Now twist the ends tighter and pull downward on the bandana and you will force the duplicate green silk slowly upward from the center of the bandana. The effect is weird in the extreme. When the silk is almost completely out, take one corner of it in your left hand and shake it out. Then remove the bandana, put the glass on the table and pass the bandana and silk for examination. The small rubber band will fall to the floor of its own accord.

8. The Vanishing Knots

EFFECT: This is a famous trick that was beautifully executed by the great Alexander Herrmann, with whom it was a favorite. The magician ties four or five silks together and then pushes them into a tube made by rolling a piece of paper and securing it with a couple of rubber bands. Some magic happens as the silks pass through the tube, for they emerge one at a time, the knots having vanished.

SECRET: The silks are tied together by means of a regulation square knot. It is a knot known to everyone, but you must practice tying it until you are certain you can always get it right, the way it is shown in the accompanying drawing.

After you tie each knot, take the part C in one hand and the end A in the other, and pull on each part, as

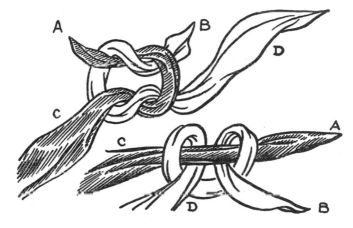

though tightening the knot. This will "upset" the knot as shown in the second drawing. A very slight pull will now slip the two loops free of part A–C and the knot will be untied.

When you push the silks into the tube, you can easily separate them with your fingers. Push them all into the tube, then shake the tube so the silks will fall out one by one.

6. More Magic with Handkerchiefs

This chapter contains tricks that are done with ordinary white pocket handkerchiefs.

1. *The Knot from Nowhere*

This is one of the best impromptu handkerchief tricks that can be done sucessfully after limited practice.

EFFECT: The magician holds a handkerchief by one corner between his right thumb and fingers. He takes in his left hand the lower corner diagonally opposite the one he is holding, brings it upward, and places it between his right thumb and fingers. With a quick snap he releases it, still holding the corner he held originally. He repeats this a second and third time, and on the third time a knot magically appears in the lower corner.

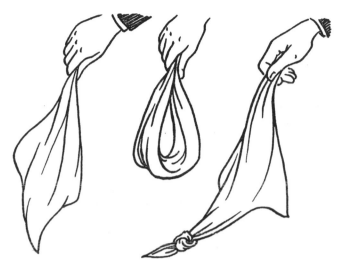

SECRET: Before doing the trick, tie a knot in one corner of the handkerchief. This corner is the one you hold
in your right hand at the beginning, the knot being hidden behind your fingers. The first two times you shake the
handkerchief out, you release the lower unknotted corner.
On the third shake, however, you keep the lower corner
in your hand and release the knotted corner.

2. The Knot That Won't Stay Tied

EFFECT: The performer ties a single knot loosely in a
handkerchief and pulls on the ends as if to tighten it. Instead the knot simply disappears.

SECRET: After you have tied the knot, put your left
thumb in the position shown in the drawing. Then grasp
the same part of the handkerchief as that which your
thumb is touching, between your left thumb and forefinger. This is done by bringing your forefinger down to

A. Your left second and third fingers hold the handkerchief as shown in the drawing. Now draw your hands quickly apart, keeping a tight hold with your left thumb and forefinger, and the knot will dissolve into thin air. Practice this a number of times and you will have a really mystifying effect.

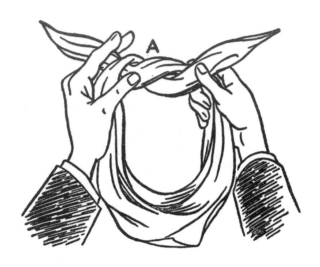

3. *The Dissolving Knots*

EFFECT: The performer takes three pocket handkerchiefs and ties them together end to end, visibly pulling the knots very tight. He then puts them behind his back and immediately produces them separated from one another, the knots having in some amazing manner disappeared.

SECRET: The handkerchiefs are tied together with regular square knots, such as the one shown in the drawing. After you tie each knot, take the part C in your left hand and the end A in your right hand, and pull hard on each part as though tightening the knot. Actually this will arrange the knot as in the second drawing and you can easily slip the two loops free of the part A–C.

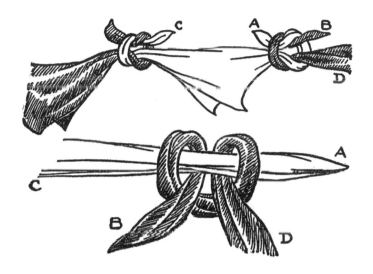

7. Magic with String

1. Ring on a String

EFFECT: The two ends of a piece of string are tied together to form a loop, a ring is threaded onto the loop, and the ends of the loop are put over a spectator's forefinger. The magician then proceeds to remove the ring without taking the string from the spectator's fingers.

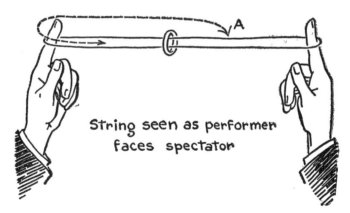

String seen as performer faces spectator

SECRET: To remove the ring, take the string which is on the side nearest the spectator's body, marked A in the drawing, grasping it to the right of the key. Move this string over to the spectator's right forefinger and make a loop around the finger, being careful to start the loop on the side of the finger that is toward the spectator, as indicated by the dotted line. Now slip off the loop that was

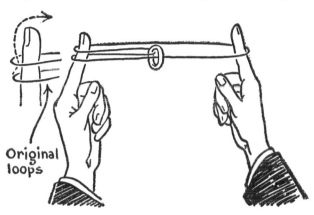

originally around the spectator's right forefinger and the ring will be released. In slipping off the original loop, bring it up *inside* the second loop, as in the second drawing. If you bring it up outside the second loop, the ring will be knotted to the string.

2. *The String in the Buttonhole*

EFFECT: The magician takes a loop of string and passes it through a buttonhole in his coat, hooking his thumbs in the two ends of the loop. With a sudden movement, the string is released from the buttonhole, although the two thumbs are still in the loops and apparently have never been removed.

SECRET: The thumbs are passed through the loops at each end of the string from the bottom upwards, as in the

first drawing. Now to release the string, hook your right little finger under the string which is nearest to it of the two strings running from the left thumb to the buttonhole, as in the second drawing. The left little finger is then hooked in the corresponding string running from the right thumb to the buttonhole.

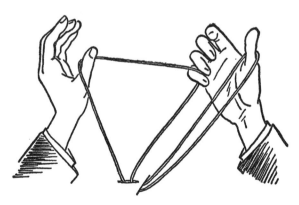

Slip the right thumb out of its loop and into the loop held by the right little finger, which is drawn well over to the right to make this movement easy. As the thumb is inserted, the right little finger is withdrawn. Immediately slip the left little finger out of its loop and draw your thumbs apart to right and left. The string will come free of the buttonhole, the effect being that it is pulled right through the fabric of your coat.

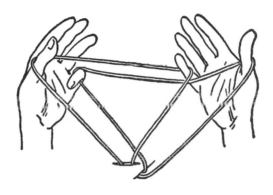

3. *Threading the Needle*

EFFECT: The magician winds a piece of stout cord upwards around his left thumb and forms a loop with the upper end, which he holds between his left thumb and

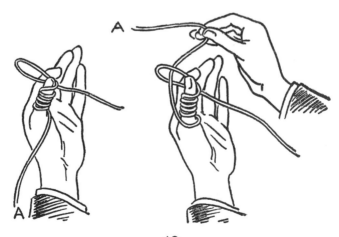

A

A

forefinger, as in the drawing. He then takes the lower end of the string A between his right thumb and forefinger and states that he is going to try to thread it through the loop without letting go of it. It is obviously impossible to do this, but after one or two quick lunges he succeeds and the string is threaded right through the loop as in the second drawing.

SECRET: This trick is quite sensational in effect, but is very easy to do. You do not really thread end A through the loop. Instead, you simply pull upward on end A and let the string slip up between your left thumb and forefinger into the loop. Try it and you will see how easily it works and how mystifying is the result.

4. Instantaneous Knot Vanish

EFFECT: A spectator is asked to tie a single overhand knot in the center of a piece of heavy cord and then to tie the ends of the cord together with several knots. The magician then states that he is going to try to untie the

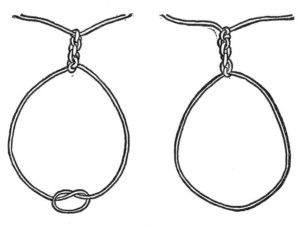

knot in the center without untying the two ends of the string. Although this is an obvious impossibility, the magician turns his back for a moment and when he turns around, shows the string with no knot in its center.

SECRET: The trick is done very simply, but in spite of this, the effect is always very surprising. All you have to do to "untie" the knot is to loosen it a little and slide it up to where the two ends of the cord are tied together. It will then merge with the other knots already there and will be soon no more in the center of the cord.

5. Thumb-and-Finger Cord Release

EFFECT: This is one of the most deceptive of all string effects and one that no spectator can do, although it looks easy and you urge whoever wants to to try it.

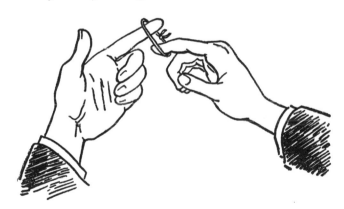

The magician takes a piece of string about 6 inches long and ties the ends together to form a loop. He then puts the loop on his forefingers, as in the first drawing, and revolves his hands several times. Stopping, he puts his thumbs and forefingers together and the loop drops away clear of his hands.

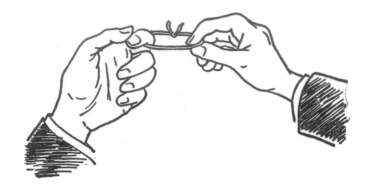

SECRET: The drawings show the way the trick is done. After revolving your hands a few times as in the first drawing, stop and place the forefinger of each hand on the tip of the thumb of the same hand, as in the second

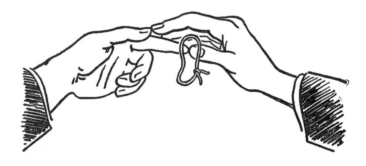

drawing. Move the hands so the left thumb and right forefinger are uppermost, then put the left thumb and right forefinger together and the left forefinger and the right thumb together, as in the third drawing. Raise the left thumb and right forefinger and the loop will be released.

6. The Thumb Tie

EFFECT: The magician has a spectator tie his two thumbs tightly together with a piece of heavy cord. Ap-

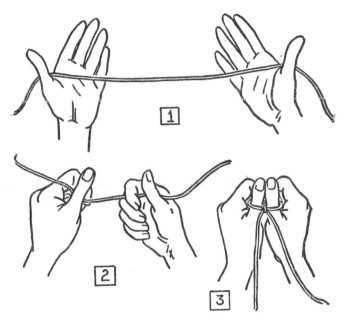

parently it is impossible for him to draw his hands apart. He succeeds in doing this instantaneously, however, and slips one arm through the arm of a person standing near him or through a loop, yet when he reunites his hands his thumbs are as tightly tied together as before. A favorite trick with some professional magicians is to have spectators toss hoops at them, which they catch on their arms and then show their thumbs still tied tightly together.

SECRET: The trick is done as follows. Hold your hands palm upward in front of you with the string to be used for tying the thumbs lying across them, passing across the palms, but between the first finger and thumb of each hand. Drawing 1. Then bring your hands together, bending in the fingers toward the wrists, and as you do so slip the tip of your right forefinger between the string and the right thumb. Drawing 2. This gives you enough slack, after your thumbs are tied together, to enable you to release yourself instantly whenever you wish to.

8. Magic with Ropes

1. The Magic Knots

EFFECT: The magician coils a rope several yards long on his left hand. He utters a few magic words, and draws the rope out to full length by one end. Knots have been magically tied in it.

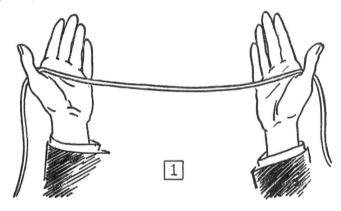

SECRET: This is an exceptionally mystifying trick and a favorite with many professional magicians. The secret is in the way the coils are made.

Start by placing the rope over your hands, with the palms held upward as in the drawing. Close the right hand over the rope and turn it palm downward, forming a loop. Drawing 2. Put this loop over the left hand, held in the position shown in the third drawing. Turn the right hand palm upward and move it along the rope to a point at which you can make a second loop. Turn the right hand over and bring this second loop to the left hand and put

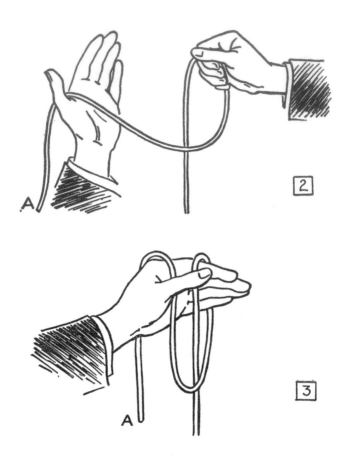

it beside the first. Continue making loops in the same way until you come to the end.

To form the knots, pass your right hand through all the loops, grasp end A, and draw it out to the right. The knots will then tie themselves, producing a very uncanny effect. Some performers, after pulling end A through all the loops, like to put the rope in a box or basket on the table. Then, after uttering the magic words, they seize end A and draw the rope slowly out of the receptacle. This does serve to heighten the effect.

2. Handkerchiefs and Ropes

EFFECT: The magician produces two pieces of rope or white sash cord, each about five feet long. Holding them side by side at their center, he has two spectators tie three handkerchiefs around them. He then passes the two right hand ends of the ropes through a cardboard mailing tube (or a glass tube such as a gas chimney). The tube is brought to the center of the ropes where it covers the handkerchiefs. Spectators then take the opposite ends of the ropes and the magician tells them to pull on them, while he holds the tube. At once, in some magical way, the tube containing the handkerchiefs is released from the ropes.

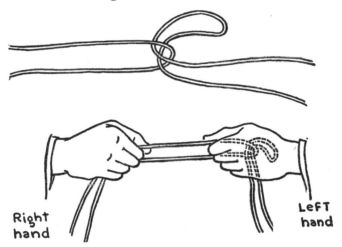

SECRET: At the beginning of the trick, show the audience the ropes and then hold them over your left hand, the ends hanging down evenly on each side. Ask two spectators to assist you and, during the diversion made by their getting up and reaching you, double the middles of the ropes as in the drawing. Do this by taking the middle of the outside rope with the right thumb and forefinger and pushing it through the bend in the other rope. Then press the left thumb on the joint, hiding it completely.

Now hold the ropes as in the second drawing, with the joints concealed by your left hand. Ask a spectator to wrap his handkerchief several times around the parts of the ropes between your hands and to tie it tightly. Turn to the other spectator and as you do so slide your left hand along the ropes and cover the joint with your right thumb. Have the second spectator tie his handkerchief on the ropes so that the hidden joint is between the two

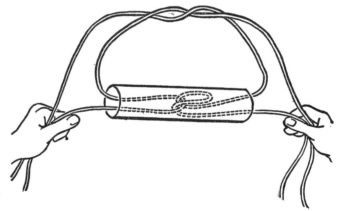

handkerchiefs. Slide the second one over the joint and have a third handkerchief tied on. Then push the two outside ones against the middle one.

Pass the two ends of the cords on one side through the tube and move it to the middle over the handkerchiefs. Then have a spectator take the opposite ends of one of the ropes and tie them in a single knot over the tube. The two spectators then hold the opposite ends of the ropes and the magician asks them to pull sharply. This undoes the joint and the tube containing the handkerchiefs drops off into the magician's hands.

The principle of this trick is an old and famous one. It is the tying of the single knot in the ropes that makes the dissolution of the joint a possibility.

3. *Cutting a Person in Two with Ropes*

EFFECT: The magician shows two pieces of rope or sash cord, each about ten feet long, and then asks for a spectator to assist him. The ropes are passed up under the assistant's coat, behind his body, and the ends are given to two spectators to hold. The magician takes a rope from each of the spectators and ties them in a single knot, across the assistant's chest. The ends are then given back to the two spectators.

The magician may now explain that this is a parlor version of sawing a woman in two or give some other explanation of what is about to happen. In any event, he tells the audience that they are about to witness something that will give them a big surprise. He asks the assistant to take two steps backward. He does so and the ropes seemingly pass right through his body. At the beginning they were behind him. Now they are in front of him.

SECRET: The principle employed is the same as that used in the last trick, but the ropes, instead of having their middles bent around each other, are fastened together with thread, as in the drawing. They are then placed on the table before the performance.

When doing the trick, pick up the ropes, covering their joined centers with your left hand. The ends will hang down naturally and the audience will have no reason to suspect that they are prepared. When your assistant

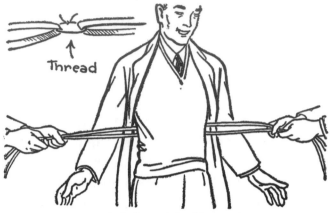

comes up, put your left hand holding the ropes up under his coat and behind his back. Then reach under his coat with your right hand and draw the two ends of the right-hand rope out to the right.

Ask two spectators to hold the opposite ends of the ropes. Then take an end from each spectator, tie a single

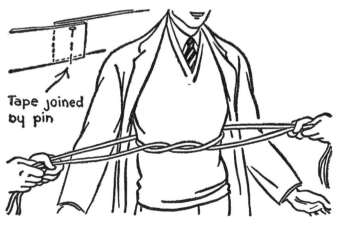

knot across your assistant's chest, and return the ends to the two spectators. Each now holds one end of each rope. Tell the assistant to step backward. This breaks the thread joining the two ropes and they immediately appear in front of him, stretched across his chest.

NOTE: There is a drawback to the trick as first described. Namely, you are not able to show the two ropes separately. This can be overcome by using two lengths of sewing tape, instead of ropes, and joining them by a pin. Have the pin in readiness, stuck in the lower part of your vest. Then, after showing the tapes separately, double back their middles and join them with the pin. This can be done while the audience's attention is drawn to your assistant as he prepares to leave his seat to join you.

4. The Knotted Loop

EFFECT: The magician holds a loop of rope between his hands, blows on it, and instantaneously a knot appears in the loop's center. This is an excellent sleight which can be done without detection right in front of everybody.

SECRET: The drawings show the steps followed in tying the knot. With a little practice you can do them in a fraction of a second. The rope is first held as in drawing 1. The first move is to turn the left hand toward you until it is in the position in drawing 2. Next slide the left hand around the inside of the loop to the position shown in drawing 3. Reach over and grasp the part of the rope marked A in your left fingers as in drawing 4. Draw the left hand to the left and through the loop that encircles

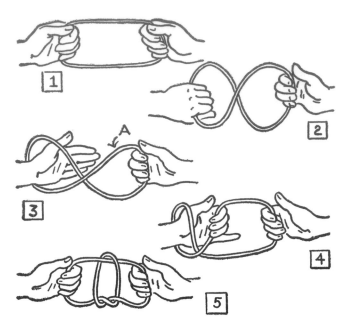

the left hand. This movement forms the magic knot, which appears in drawing 5.

5. *Two Instantaneous Knots*

EFFECT: The magician holds a piece of rope about four feet long, one end in each hand. A rapid movement, and two knots appear in the rope.

SECRET: Hold the ends of the rope in each hand, backs of the hands upward. With your right hand throw about 2½ feet of the rope over the left wrist to form a loop about 15 inches long. This hangs down outside your left wrist. See drawing. Pass the right hand, holding its end of the rope, away from you and through the loop in an outward direction. Then draw the hands apart as far as they will go.

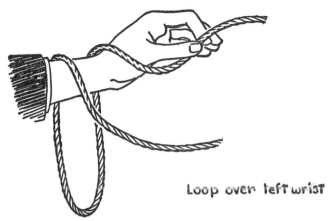

Loop over left wrist

Revolve the left wrist toward yourself, under the ropes, and on to its original position. Exchange ends of the ropes, taking in your left hand the end originally held by the right, and vice versa. Be sure to pass the original right end inside the left end, so that it is next to your body and the left end is outside it. Slip your hands out of the loops and pull your hands apart, and two knots will be formed in the middle of the rope.

6. *The Stretching Rope*

EFFECT: The magician shows a piece of rope about three feet long, which he holds in his right hand. Taking one end in his left hand, he pulls on it and the rope stretches out until it is 10 feet long. This trick is also done by having a spectator pull on one end and draw the rope out.

SECRET: One piece of rope 10 feet long is used. It should be soft and pliable. To prepare for the trick, re-

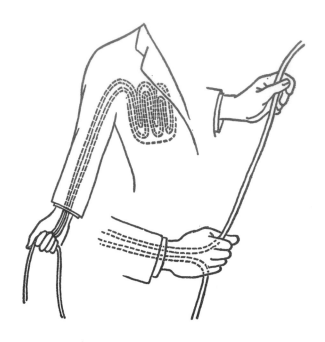

move your coat, take both ends of the rope in your right hand and put on the coat, drawing the rope ends down the sleeve. The looped center of the rope will now be hanging down inside your coat. Fold it up in zigzag loops and put it in the inside pocket of the coat on the right side.

In doing the trick, this preparation must be done off stage, and the trick must be the first one you do. Enter, holding the ends of the rope in the right hand, as shown in the drawing. Take the left end in your left hand, hold that hand motionless, and move the right hand away. When the hands are a few feet apart, drop the rope from the left hand, move the two hands close together, and take the rope again in your left hand. Continue the motions until the rope is out of your right sleeve.

9. Mind-Reading Magic

1. Dictionary or Book Mind Reading

EFFECT: This trick is done with an assistant who is described as being extremely sensitive to telepathic mental vibrations. He goes into an adjoining room and the performer then gives a small dictionary or book to a spectator. The spectator is asked to choose a word or a sentence but not to name it; merely give the page and the number of the word (if a dictionary) or the sentence on the page. The spectator then concentrates on his word or sentence and in a few moments the assistant tells what it is.

SECRET: This is an exceptionally good trick. It is done by using duplicate small dictionaries of the kind that can be bought at the ten-cent store, or duplicate books, such as 25-cent reprints. The assistant has one book in his pocket and when he hears the number of the page and the number of the word or sentence on the page, looks it up and in due course reads it aloud.

85

2. *The Chosen Number*

EFFECT: In this mind-reading experiment the performer is blindfolded and taken to another room while the spectators select a number between 1 and 10. The performer then returns and places his hands one on each side of his assistant's forehead, "in order to receive his thought waves more readily." No word is spoken, but the performer quickly announces the chosen number.

SECRET: The method used to transmit the number to the performer is very clever and works on a little-known principle. The assistant simply puts his teeth together and clamps his jaws the proper number of times to indicate the chosen number. The performer, with his hands on the assistant's temples, can easily feel the movements of the bone.

3. The Chosen Card

EFFECT: Twelve cards are dealt out in a row on the table and the "mind reader" leaves the room while the audience selects one of them. When the performer returns, his assistant points silently to one card after another. The performer says, "no," until the chosen card is pointed out, when he at once states it to be the one chosen by the audience.

SECRET: The assistant indicates the chosen card to the performer by pointing to it immediately after he has pointed to one of the cards which is next to either end of the row.

4. Book Mind Reading

This is a mind-reading effect that will mystify any audience. Provided you have an assistant with you who knows the secret, it can be performed at a moment's notice at a party or other gathering where you are asked to do some magic.

EFFECT: The mind reader's assistant is blindfolded and seated on a chair and the performer then carries a book to the spectators and asks one of them to insert a playing card or a small piece of cardboard like a visiting card in the book at any place he desires. The book is then opened at the page at which the card was inserted and the mind reader asks his assistant to tell the number of the page and to read the first line of print. After a few moments of concentration the assistant succeeds in carrying out this seemingly impossible feat. He is aided, of course, by the performer and the spectators reading and concentrating on the page and the words to convey them telepathically to the assistant's mind.

SECRET: This astonishing mind-reading effect is done as follows. Prior to the performance, the mind reader and his assistant select a certain page in the book that is to be used. The assistant memorizes the page number and the first line. A playing card or a small piece of cardboard similar to the one that is later given to the spectator is then inserted in this page.

When presenting the trick, the performer holds the book so the secret card is in the end nearest his body and so invisible to the audience. The spectator then inserts the card given to him in the opposite end. When he has done so, the performer turns away for a moment to face his assistant or walk back toward his table. At this point he turns the books around so the secret card marking the memorized page is toward the audience. At the same time the spectator's card is pushed well out of sight inside the book. Now, of course, when the book is opened to the page indicated by the secret card, it will be the page previously selected by the mind reader and his assistant.

5. Dollar-Bill Mind Reading

EFFECT: The "mind reader" sits in a chair and his assistant borrows several dollar bills from the audience. He does not utter a word or go near the mind reader, but holds the bills one at a time in his hand and concentrates on the serial number, sending his thought waves to the magician. The latter calls out the serial numbers on the bills, writing them down on pieces of paper to check against the bills themselves.

SECRET: This trick is done by means of a very clever and undetectable finger code. The numbers from 0 to 9 are indicated as follows.

Zero=The assistant holds the bill by the top edge.

1=The assistant holds the end of the bill in his right hand with the thumb in back and the forefinger slightly extended across the face of the bill.

2=The bill is held in the same way as for number 1 but with the first and second fingers extended.

3=Same as before but with three fingers extended.

4=Same as before but with all four fingers extended.

5=The assistant holds the bill by the bottom edge.

6=The assistant holds the bill in his left hand with the forefinger extended across the face.

7=Same as for number 6 but with the first and second fingers extended.

8=Same as before but with three fingers extended.

9=Same as before but with all four fingers extended.

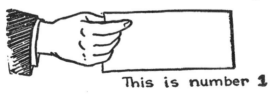

This is number 1

This is number 2

Take a bill and "spell out" the serial number by this code. You will find that the shift from one signal to the next can be made very naturally. Also, when the right hand, for example, is signaling, the left hand can also hold the bill, but with the fingers curled up. Do not hurry this trick. Let the performer get the numbers and write them down one by one, the short spaces between each number being occupied by concentration.

6. Diabolo Dictionary Trick

EFFECT: This is one of the most surprising of all mind-reading tricks. Briefly the effect is as follows: Ten pieces of paper are given to ten spectators with the request that they write down any number between 1 and 300. The papers are folded, collected, and placed in a glass on the performer's table. Ten more pieces of paper are passed out and the people receiving them are asked to write down any number between 1 and 50. These are folded, collected, and placed in a hat.

The performer takes the glass and asks a spectator to draw out one of the pieces of paper and to read aloud the number written on it. It is, say, 149. Another spectator draws a paper from the hat and reads out, say, the number 32. The performer then gives a dictionary to the audience and asks them to turn to page 149 and count down to the 32d word. The spectators are asked to concentrate on this word and the performer closes his eyes to concentrate. In a few moments he writes a word on a piece of paper and gives it to a spectator to read aloud. It is the same word as the one found in the dictionary by the audience.

SECRET: The effect of this trick is really startling, but the method of doing it is very simple. Before the performance, write the number 149 (or some other number between 1 and 300) on ten small pieces of paper. Fold them and put a loose-fitting rubber band around them and put them in a lower vest pocket. Write the number 32 (or some number between 1 and 50) on ten other pieces of paper, fold them, place a rubber band around them, and put them in your other lower vest pocket.

When you collect the first set of ten papers, those with the numbers between 1 and 300, take them in your right hand. When you turn to go back to your table, put these papers in the vest pocket containing the secret papers on each of which is written 149. At the same time take out the secret papers. When you reach your table, drop the secret papers in the glass.

The second set of papers is handled in the same way, the secret ones bearing the number 32 being placed in the hat. Now, the spectators who take papers from the glass and the hat are bound to get the numbers 149 and 32. The word that you write down is the 32d word on the 149th page in the dictionary. You have looked this word up and memorized it, of course, before presenting the trick.

10. Magic with Dice

1. Dice Divination

EFFECT: This is an effective and interesting trick which always impresses an audience, even though it is understood that it is worked entirely by mathematical principles. In doing it, the performer leaves the room, one of the spectators throws two dice on a table, and the performer then tells him what number he has thrown.

SECRET: The trick is done by the following arithmetical steps. As soon as the dice have been thrown, the performer asks the spectator to take the uppermost number on either one of the dice and multiply it by 2, then add 5 to the product and multiply the sum thus obtained by 5. The last step is to add the uppermost number on the other die to this figure. When the performer is told the total, he at once announces the number of spots uppermost on each of the dice.

The only calculating that you have to do is to subtract 25 from the last total arrived at by the person who threw the dice. This will give you a two-number figure. One of these numbers will be the same as the number of spots uppermost on one of the dice, and the other figure will indicate the spots uppermost on the other dice. As an example, if the total obtained by the spectator is 52, you would subtract 25 and get 27. One of these dice would have 2 spots uppermost and the other one 7 spots.

2. Magnetic Dice

EFFECT: The magician takes two dice and places one on top of the other. After making a few magnetic magic passes, he takes hold of the top one and raises it. In some mysterious manner the bottom die clings to it, magnetized, as the magician explains. The dice are then separated and shown to be unprepared and free of wax or any other adhesive material.

SECRET: A little moisture applied to the bottom surface of the upper die is the method used in this trick. The top of the right thumb or forefinger is secretly moistened with the tongue and then applied to the die.

By pressing down firmly when putting the top die in place, it will adhere to the lower die and bring it along with it when it is lifted.

3. Naming Unseen Die Spots

EFFECT: While the magician turns his back, three dice are set one on top of the other by the audience. The magician then turns around and immediately tells the total of the spots on the tops and bottoms of the two lower dice and the bottom of the third and uppermost die. All these spots are, of course, concealed from the magician's view.

SECRET: If you will examine a die, you will see that the spots on any two opposite sides always total 7. Thus the totals of the tops and bottoms of all three dice would be 21. To name the total of the hidden spots as described above, all you have to do is to subtract the number of spots on the top of the uppermost die from 21.

4. The Dice in the Glass

EFFECT: The magician gives three dice and a drinking glass to a spectator and asks him to drop the dice into the glass. The magician then names the spots on the bottom surfaces of the dice, and when the glass is held up above eye level, his prediction or divination is found to be correct.

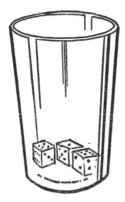

SECRET: Since, as explained in "Naming Unseen Die Spots," the total of all three tops and bottoms will be 21, you simply add the spots showing on the tops of the dice, and subtract this sum from 21. This will give you the total of the spots on the bottom surfaces of the three dice.

5. *Dice Mathemagic*

EFFECT: A spectator throws three dice on a table and adds together the uppermost spots. The magician, who is blindfolded, picks up one of the dice and asks the spectator to add the number of spots on the side nearest him to the total already obtained. Throwing this die on the table, the magician asks the spectator to add the spots now on its uppermost side to his previous figure. He then removes the blindfold, looks at the dice as they lie on the table, and at once announces the total figure computed by the spectator.

SECRET: The secret of this trick lies in the fact that you show the spectator the reverse or bottom side of the die that you pick up. If this is done, the spectator's total can always be discovered by adding 7 to the total of the uppermost spots of the dice as they lie on the table when you remove the blindfold.

11. Thimble Magic

Thimble tricks are invariably interesting and provide a welcome variety to any program of magic. Ordinary thimbles purchased at a ten-cent store are used. For better visibility they may be painted red or blue.

1. *The Disappearing Thimble*

EFFECT: This trick involves one of the basic thimble sleights, which is practically the same as the thumb grip used with coins. The magician puts a thimble on his right

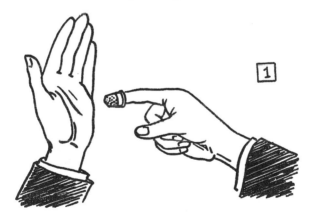

fingertip and apparently removes it with his left hand. When the left hand is opened, however, the thimble has vanished. Both hands are then shown empty.

SECRET: The vanish is executed as follows. The right forefinger is extended, pointing to the left. The left hand

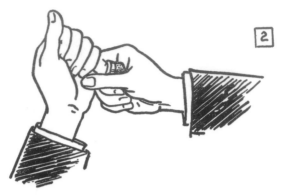

then approaches it and closes over it, but under cover of the left fingers, the right forefinger is quickly doubled in and the thimble is tucked into the crook of the thumb. The left hand is then withdrawn, being kept closed as though it held the thimble. Turn your left side to the spectators and drop the thimble behind some object on your table or into one of your right-hand pockets.

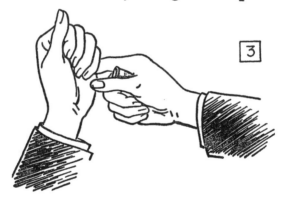

2. *The Flying Thimble*

EFFECT: The performer places a thimble on the tip of his right forefinger and makes a tossing or passing motion toward his left hand. Quick as a flash the thimble

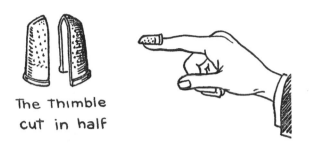

The Thimble
cut in half

vanishes, only to reappear instantly on his left forefinger. The thimble is then passed from hand to hand several times by the same instantaneous magic.

SECRET: The trick is done with a thimble that has been cut in half from top to bottom. One half is placed on the tip of the left forefinger on the back side of the finger. Thus, when the palm of the left hand is turned toward the audience, there is nothing to be seen; but when the back of the hand is turned toward them, the thimble appears. The other half is placed on the front side of the right forefinger and is made to disappear by turning the back of the hand toward the audience.

3. The Color-Changing Thimble

EFFECT: This is a very pretty color-change effect worked with a red and a blue thimble. At the beginning, the red thimble is on the magician's right forefinger. He takes it in his left hand and immediately shows that its

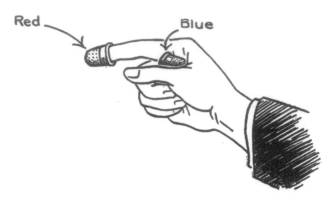

Red

Blue

color has changed to blue. One beauty of the trick is that both hands are shown empty except for the one thimble that is visible.

SECRET: At the beginning, the red thimble is on the right forefinger and the blue thimble is thumb-gripped in the right hand. The left hand is shown to be empty and is

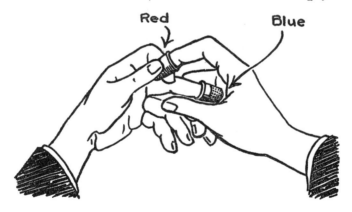

Red

Blue

then brought over toward the right hand. The left thumb and forefinger grasp the red thimble, and at the same moment the left middle finger is pushed into the blue thimble. The middle finger is then at once bent in toward the palm to keep the blue thimble out of sight.

The right hand is now shown to be empty. Next the red thimble is replaced on the right forefinger, and the blue thimble is simultaneously thumb-gripped in the left hand.

Everything is now ready for the color change. The left hand is closed and placed over the right forefinger, from which it apparently removes the red thimble. Actually the red thimble is thumb-gripped or tucked into the crook of the right thumb. The left hand is withdrawn, containing only the blue thimble which is at once revealed to the audience. As this is done, turn your left side to the audience and drop the red thimble in a pocket or behind some object on your table. Turn to face the audience and casually show your right to be empty.

4. Thimble Production from a Paper Cone

EFFECT: The magician shows a piece of writing paper, front and back, and then rolls it up into a cone or cornucopia. He shows his right hand to be empty and inserts his right forefinger into the cone. When he withdraws it, there is a thimble on its tip.

SECRET: The thimble is thumb-gripped before starting the trick. It is therefore well out of sight while the paper is being shown to the audience. When both sides of the paper have been shown, let go of it with your right hand for a moment and, under cover of the paper, get the thimble onto your right forefinger. Your left hand holds the paper while this is being done. Then take hold of the paper again with the right hand, putting the thumb in front and the forefinger behind the paper on the side toward yourself. Roll the paper into a cone around the right forefinger and leave the thimble in the cone. Casually show your right hand to be empty, put it into the cone, and bring out the thimble.

5. *The Multiplying Thimble*

EFFECT: The magician catches a thimble out of the air. It vanishes and, in a series of moves, multiplies to four thimbles, which are displayed on the tips of the right-hand fingers.

SECRET: Before doing the trick, secrete three thimbles about your person. Put one in the right side of your shirt collar, one in your left lower vest pocket, and one, mouth downward, under your belt. Other places may be used if more convenient. A fourth thimble is thumb-gripped in the right hand. The trick is to be carried out as follows.

Move your right hand swiftly upward and catch the thumb-gripped thimble "out of the air," exhibiting it on your right forefinger. Again make a tossing motion with the right hand and vanish the thimble by thumb-gripping it. Look about as though trying to see where it has gone. Then put your forefinger in your shirt collar and bring out the thimble secreted there. Remove this thimble from your right forefinger and put it on the middle finger.

Catch the thumb-gripped thimble once more on your right forefinger and show the two thimbles. Vanish this thimble and pretend to find it in your vest pocket, bringing out the thimble secreted there on your right forefinger. Remove this thimble and put it on your right third finger. Catch the thumb-gripped thimble again on your right forefinger and show the three thimbles.

Once again vanish the thimble on the right forefinger by thumb-gripping it. Discover it beneath your belt, bringing out the thimble secreted there on your forefinger. Put this thimble on your right little finger. Then produce the thumb-gripped thimble from your left elbow and hold up your hand to show all four thimbles.

6. From Red to Blue

EFFECT: The performer shows a red thimble which he puts on the tip of his right forefinger. He takes the thimble in his left hand, which he keeps closed for a moment. When the hand is opened, the thimble is found to have changed color. It is now blue.

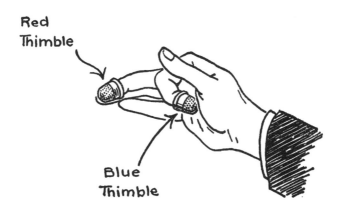

Red
Thimble

Blue
Thimble

SECRET: Two thimbles are used, one red and one blue. At the beginning the blue one is thumb-gripped in the right hand.

Pick up the red thimble from the table and put it on the right middle finger. Extend this finger, with the other fingers folded into the palm. As you fold the fingers in,

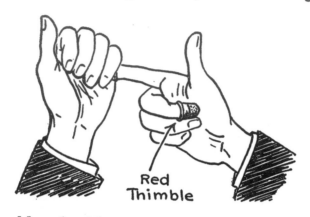

Red
Thimble

get the blue thimble on the tip of the right forefinger. See drawing.

Move the right hand toward the left and apparently remove the red thimble with the left hand, which is closed around the finger. Actually, just as the two hands approach each other, the middle finger is bent in and the red thimble is thumb-gripped. At the same instant, the right forefinger is extended, the blue thimble on its tip being hidden by the left hand. The left hand closes over and removes the blue thimble. After a moment the left hand is opened and the blue thimble is revealed. At this moment you can get rid of the red thimble by turning your left side to the audience and dropping the red thimble onto your table or into a pocket. The lower right-hand vest pocket is a good one to use for this move.

7. Thimble and Handkerchief

EFFECT: The magician puts a thimble on his right forefinger and covers it with a handkerchief. He reaches under the handkerchief and removes the thimble, which he places on his forefinger on top of the handkerchief. Thus the handkerchief is between the thimble and the tip of the forefinger. With a rapid movement the magician pulls the handkerchief away. To everyone's astonishment, the thimble stays right on the finger, the handkerchief having apparently passed right through it.

SECRET: Two thimbles are used, one a little larger than the other. They are fitted together and are placed on the right forefinger where they look like a single thimble. After the handkerchief is placed over the right hand, you reach under it and withdraw the larger thimble, placing it over the finger on top of the handkerchief.

When you whisk away the handkerchief, do not hold it by one corner, but gather up all four corners in the left hand. This forms the handkerchief into a kind of bag in which the larger thimble is caught when the handkerchief is removed.

8. Thimble and Paper-Cone Finale

This is a beautiful trick with which to conclude a series of three or four thimble effects. It is little known and always produces a remarkable effect.

EFFECT: A thimble is shown on the tip of the right forefinger. It vanishes and reappears under a small paper cone that the performer has placed on his table. Again

Cone

Two
nested
thimbles

the thimble vanishes and finds its way under the cone, and the invisible flight is then repeated a third time.

SECRET: Two thimbles, one a little larger than the other, are used. These are fitted together and are put on the tip of the right forefinger. Remove the thimbles and make a small paper cone, just large enough to fit easily over the thimbles. Have the edge of the open mouth of the cone even, so it will stand upright on the table with the point upward.

Put the thimbles back on the right forefinger for a moment, and put the cone over them, as though to see whether it fits. As you remove the cone, also remove the larger thimble. Put the cone on your table, with the thimble inside it. It is best to have a cloth on the table so the thimble will make no noise.

Pretend to take the remaining thimble in your left hand, but really thumb-grip it in the right hand. Pass the closed left hand over the cone a few times; then open the left hand and show it to be empty. Lift the cone, not by the point but by the mouth or the lower edge, with the right hand, and show the thimble beneath it. While the spectators' attention is on this thimble, let the thumb-gripped thimble drop into the cone. Put the cone back on the table with the new thimble beneath it.

Take the exposed thimble from the table and place it on the right forefinger. Make an upward tossing motion with the right hand and vanish the thimble by thumb-gripping it. Pick up the cone again, but this time grip it between the first and second fingers of the right hand. See drawing. Point to the thimble on the table with your left forefinger. As you do so, turn the cone, mouth upward, toward the inside of the right hand and let the

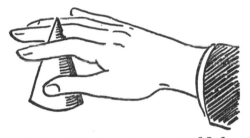

thumb-gripped thimble drop into it. Hold the cone mouth upward with the thimble in it. Try this move and you will find that it can be done quickly, easily, and without any untoward movement that would attract attention.

Take the cone in the left hand, holding it by the point. Put the thimble from the table on your right forefinger and vanish it by making a tossing motion with the hand and thumb gripping the thimble. Look upward, as though watching the flight of the thimble, then move the left hand quickly forward, holding the cone as though to catch the thimble in the cone. Glance into the cone and then hold it out to a spectator, asking him to hold out his hand. Turn the cone over and let the thimble drop into his hand. While doing this, turn your left side to the audience and drop the other thimble into your right-hand vest or trouser pocket.

12. Dinner-Table Magic

1. The Wandering Bread Pellets

EFFECT: Seated at the dinner table, the performer rolls up small pieces of bread to form three pellets, each about the size of a pea. He vanishes one of the pellets and it appears under a plate or napkin placed in readiness on the table. He vanishes the second and third pellets and they appear beside the first one. The pellets are then invisibly transported one by one and appear under a second plate or napkin placed nearby.

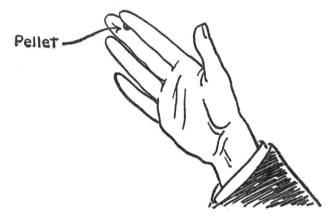

Pellet

SECRET: Well done, this is a sure-fire mystifier. To start with, you make four pellets instead of the three you show your audience. The fourth one is held between the first and second fingers of the right hand. Pick up two plates or napkins and in putting them back on the table beside each other, drop the fourth pellet under the right-hand plate. This is easily done if you hold the plate with the fingers underneath and the thumb on top.

Take one of the three visible pellets and pretend to throw it into the air, but really nip it between your right-hand fingers. Pick up the right-hand plate and reveal the pellet already there. Replace the plate, secretly dropping the pellet in your right fingers. Throw the second pellet into the air and reveal it under the plate as before. Repeat with the third pellet.

You now have three pellets under the right-hand plate and one pellet in your right fingers.

Continue by lifting the left-hand plate with your *right* hand. Show that there is nothing beneath the left-hand plate. Replace it and drop the pellet in your right hand beneath it. Pick up the right-hand plate and show the three pellets beneath it. As you replace it, grip one of the pellets between your right fingers. With both hands make a motion from right to left as though passing a pellet from plate to plate. Lift the left-hand plate with your right hand and show the pellet under it. As you replace the plate, drop the pellet in your right fingers beneath it. Pick up the right-hand plate and show that only two pellets remain under it. As you replace it, nip one of the pellets between your right fingers. Transfer this pellet to the left-hand plate as before, and then transfer the third pellet in the same way.

2. Pellets from Hand to Hand

EFFECT: The magician makes two small pellets of bread. He puts one on the table and puts the other one in his left hand. Picking up the one on the table, he puts it in a spectator's hand. He then commands the pellet in his own hand to join the one held by the spectator. When he opens his left hand, it is seen to be empty. The spectator opens his hand and discovers the two pellets there.

SECRET: This trick is done with two pellets only. At the start when you appear to put one pellet in the left hand, you really nip it between the first and second

fingers of the right hand. Immediately close the left hand, and the illusion of the pellet really being placed within it is perfect.

Pick up the second pellet and hold it between the tips of your right thumb and first and second fingers. Ask a spectator to hold out his hand. Put the visible pellet on his palm and drop the other pellet also. Do this slowly and deliberately, talking steadily, describing what you are doing. This will take attention away from your right hand. Keep your right-hand thumb and fingers on the spectator's palm for several moments while you are talking. Then tell him, "Close your hand, please, and keep it closed for a few moments."

Conclude the trick quite rapidly by opening your own left hand and telling the spectator to open his, so he will not have time to feel the two pellets in his hand.

3. *The Midas Dinner Roll*

EFFECT: The magician picks up a roll and turns it around in his hands, as though speculating what to do with it. In a moment he says, "This roll seems to be a little heavy. Perhaps there is something in it." He breaks it open and imbedded in the center is a quarter.

SECRET: Before starting the trick, palm the coin in your right hand, gripping it in the center of the palm as in the drawing. As you turn the roll over and over, get the coin to your fingertips and hold it beneath the roll. If the roll is fairly soft, you can push the coin into it. If it is hard,

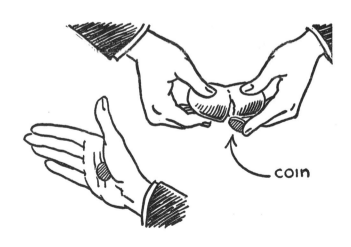

coin

111

take it by the ends and press them so as to break the roll on its lower side. Push the coin into the opening with your fingers. Then break the roll on its upper side, separate it into two pieces, and reveal the coin.

4. The Impromptu Drinking Cup

EFFECT: Seated at the dinner table, the magician takes a paper napkin or a cloth napkin (or a dollar bill) and rolls it into a small tube. Picking up a glass of water, he pours some into the tube, from which he drinks it, remarking that a napkin or a bill always makes water taste better.

SECRET: This is done with the aid of a thumb tip, which is one of the magician's most indispensable adjuncts. Dinner-table tricks must be prepared for just as much as stage tricks, and if you become really interested in magic you will soon acquire a thumb tip and carry it about with you.

In this trick you roll up the napkin around your right thumb, upon which you have previously placed a thumb tip. Leave the thumb tip inside the tube. Take the tube in the left hand, pour a little water into the thumb tip, and drink the water. Unroll the tube, bringing your right hand over to do so, and putting your right thumb inside to pick up the thumb tip, under cover of the fingers of both hands.

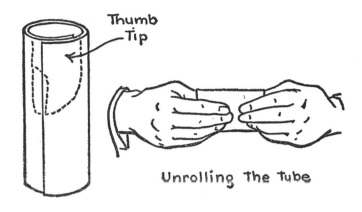

Thumb Tip

Unrolling the tube

5. The Mysterious Fruit Seed

EFFECT: The magician takes an apple or grape seed from fruit that is on the table or produces a seed from his pocket. Pouring a glass of ginger ale or soda water, he drops the seed into it, and it sinks to the bottom. He commands it to rise to the top of the glass and it immediately does so. The magician waves his hand downward and the seed sinks to the bottom, only to rise to the surface again when the magician orders it to do so.

113

SECRET: The seed first sinks, and then rises to the surface because bubbles or gas adhere to it and cause it to float upward. At the surface the bubbles burst and the seed sinks to the bottom, but rises again when it accumulates more bubbles. You should try this trick out privately before showing it, so you will know the timing of the seed's rising and falling.

6. *The Drinking-glass Vanish*

EFFECT: This is a wonder when well done and has a startling climax. The magician puts a coin on the dinner table, sets a drinking glass over it mouth downward, and says that he is going to pass the coin through the glass. He puts a piece of newspaper over the glass and puts a napkin around the newspaper. Then, totally unexpectedly, he strikes down at the glass with his fist. The newspaper crushes down and the glass has disappeared.

Putting
the newspaper
over the glass —

114

SECRET: Putting the glass over the coin is simply misdirection. You do not wish to tell the audience that you are going to vanish the glass, so you tell them you are going to do something else.

To do the trick, put a coin on the table, put a glass near it and say that you are going to try to make the coin pass through the glass. Press several sheets of newspaper down over the glass, shaping them to the cylindrical form of the glass. Now put the glass over the coin, but apparently change your mind and move the glass close to the edge of the table at which you are sitting. Explain this by saying that the trick is rather surprising and the glass sometimes breaks. You do not want anyone to be hurt by the flying pieces.

While talking, shape the napkin around the newspaper and slowly move the covered glass to the edge of the table. Then let it drop into your lap. Move the newspaper and napkin back over the coin. The newspaper will stand up and retain the shape of the glass. Now raise your right fist and bring it down swiftly. The newspaper will flatten out and the glass will have gone.

Striking
the glass

One way to conclude the trick is to have someone crawl under the table and find the glass there some distance from yourself. You can do this by letting the glass slide from your lap down your outstretched legs. If you prefer, you can let the glass roll or drop to the floor and leave it there, while you pass on to another trick.

7. *Drinking-glass Levitation*

EFFECT: The magician puts his hand across the top of a glass that is nearly full of water. He raises his hand and the glass, adhering to his palm, is lifted off the table.

SECRET: The glass adheres to your hand because you create a partial vacuum underneath the hand. You do this by putting the palm of your hand squarely over the top of the glass and bending the fingers at a right angle, as in the first drawing. Now, still applying the palm with some force to the glass, suddenly stretch out your fingers so as to give the palm its utmost tension. This will create a partial vacuum that will be great enough to make the glass adhere to your palm.

13. Stunts to Fool Your Friends

Stunts and gags are always good for a laugh or, as they are often employed, to win bets with. Some of the best are given here. You can use them in any way and at any time when the opportunity is ripe—at the luncheon table or at an evening party. They are sure-fire and will give your friends some good laughs as well as something to puzzle about.

1. Odd or Even Serial Numbers

Ask someone to take a dollar bill from his wallet, put it flat on the table, and cover the serial numbers in the lower left and upper right corners with his two thumbs. Without any trouble at all, you then proceed to tell him whether the serial number is odd or even.

This stunt is done by looking at the single letter that is printed on the face of the bill in two places, near the upper left corner and the lower right corner. This letter indicates whether the serial number is odd or even as follows: A is odd, B is even, C is odd, D is even, E is odd, and so on.

2. Reverse Shift

This is a tricky one that is easy when you know how, but a sticker for the uninitiated.

Make a triangle with ten pennies, as in the drawing. Then ask a friend if he can shift three of the pennies so the triangle will be reversed and will point down instead of up.

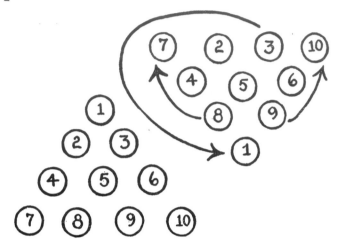

To reverse the triangle, shift penny 7 to the left of 2, penny 10 to the right of 3, and penny 1 down to the bottom to a position beneath and between 8 and 9.

3. All Together

Put 4 pennies and 4 nickels in a row on the table, first a penny, then a nickel, and so on, so the coins alternate as shown in the drawing.

Then ask a friend to see if he can get all the pennies and all the nickels together by making four moves. In each move, two coins next to each other must be moved together, without changing their position, to a new set of two empty spaces.

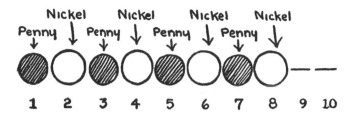

Nickel   Nickel   Nickel   Nickel

Penny ↓ Penny ↓ Penny ↓ Penny ↓

1   2   3   4   5   6   7   8   9   10

Two extra spaces, 9 and 10, are shown in the drawing, in order to make the moves clear. Move 2 and 3 to 9 and 10. Move 5 and 6 to 2 and 3. Move 8 and 9 to 5 and 6. Then move 1 and 2 to 8 and 9, and the puzzle will be solved.

4. Coin Shifting

Here is another coin-shifting stunt with which you can win bets or just amuse your friends.

Put two quarters and a nickel on the table, arranged as shown in the drawing, with the nickel between the two

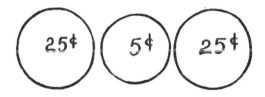

quarters. Then bet a friend that he cannot put one of the quarters in the middle, taking the place of the nickel, moving the coins in accordance with the following conditions:

The quarter at the left may be moved but not touched.
The quarter at the right may be moved and touched.
The nickel may be touched but not moved.

119

At first glance it looks impossible, but there is a way to do it, which is as follows:

Put your left middle finger firmly on the nickel. Then put your right forefinger and middle finger on the right-hand quarter, and move it to the right. Move this quarter quickly to the left against the nickel. This will cause the left-hand quarter to move to the left, and will make a space in which you can put the right-hand quarter, thus winning your bet.

5. *Penny Jumping*

Put ten pennies, or checkers, in a row on the table. Then ask a friend to see if he can do the following: pick up a penny, jump two adjoining pennies, and "crown" the next penny to make a king, as in checkers, by putting the

first penny on top of it. This would be like picking up penny 1, jumping it over 2 and 3, and putting it on penny 4. Then continue in the same way until there are only kings. When you jump over a king, count it as two checkers. You can jump both to the right and to the left.

To solve this one, put penny 4 on 1; 6 on 9; 8 on 3; 2 on 5; and 7 on 10. Five moves and it's done.

6. *Some Knot*

Hand your handkerchief to someone and tell him to hold one end in each hand. Then tell him that it is possible to hold a handkerchief in this way and, without letting go of it with either hand, to tie a single overhand knot in it. Let him try it a few times and then show him how it is done.

The secret is simple. Put the handkerchief on the table and then fold your arms across your chest. Pick up one end of the handkerchief in each hand. Then pull your arms apart and the knot will be formed in the center of the handkerchief.

7. *Pennies and Pencils*

Put nine pennies on the table arranged in three equally spaced rows of three pennies each, as in the drawing. Put four long pencils beside the pennies.

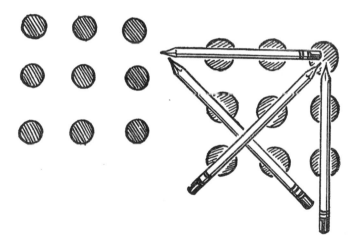

Ask someone if they can place the pencils so they will cover all nine of the pennies, with each pencil touching each of the other three pencils.

How to do it is shown in the second drawing.

8. Next Higher Number

Try this one on some friend who prides himself on his ability with figures, or else just work it on someone from whom you want to win a bet.

Tell your friend that you are going to call out some numbers and that he is to call out at once the correct next higher number. Then tell him you are pretty sure that he will not be able to carry out his part of the bargain and, if you like, make a bet with him to this effect.

Start with an easy number like 49, to which he will reply "Fifty." Then call out 99. He will say "A hundred." Follow with 999, to which the answer is "A thousand." Then give him Nine thousand ninety-nine (9099). It is ten to one that he will call out "Ten thousand." A moment's reflection will show that the correct answer is Nine thousand one hundred (9100).